GODDARD PARENTING GUIDES

Me, Myself and I

How Children Build Their Sense of Self

18 TO 36 MONTHS

Kyle D. Pruett, M.D.

GODDARD PRESS

380 MADISON AVENUE

NEW YORK, NY 10017

Copyright ©1999 by Goddard Press, Inc.

Book design by Stan Adler Associates.

Manufactured in the United States of America.

PUBLISHER'S CATALOGING-IN-PUBLICATION DATA

Pruett, Kyle D.

Me, myself and I: how children build their sense of self – 18 to 36 months

p.   cm.   (Goddard parenting guides)

Includes bibliographical references. 1. Parenting. 2. Child care.

ISBN 0-9666397-4-X

        0-9666397-5-8 (pbk)

1. Self in infants. 2. Infants — Development. 3. Parent and infant. I. Title. II. Series.

BF720.S44 P78 1999   99-60433

155.4/22--dc21   CIP

THE AUTHOR AND PUBLISHER GRATEFULLY ACKNOWLEDGE PERMISSION TO REPRINT MATERIAL FROM THE FOLLOWING WORKS AND INDIVIDUALS:

Chap. 2. PET scans reprinted by permission of Harry T. Chugani, M.D., Children's Hospital of Michigan, Wayne State University. © Harry Chugani

Chap. 2. Excerpts reprinted with permission from *Rethinking the Brain,* 1997, published by the Families and Work Institute.

Chap. 2. Excerpt reproduced by permission of *Pediatrics* 59: 388–389, © 1977.

Chap. 9. Excerpt reprinted with permission from *The NICHD Study of Early Child Care,* National Institute of Child Health and Human Development, 1998.

CHAPTER PHOTOGRAPHS: *Cover:* Bob Winsett/Index Stock Imagery, Bob Llewellyn/Uniphoto; *Chap. 1:* C/B Productions/The Stock Market; *Chap. 2:* Monica Kosann Photography; *Chap. 3:* Carlos Saito/Photonica; *Chap. 4:* Rob Goldman; *Chap. 5:* John Russell Photography, Inc.; *Chap. 6:* Picture Perfect; *Chap. 7:* Elizabeth Hathan; *Chap. 8:* Mug Shots/The Stock Market; *Chap. 9:* David Stoecklein/The Stock Market; *Chap. 10:* Allan Luftig; *Pg. 186:* Lars Klove/The Image Bank; *Pg. 187:* George Shelley/The Stock Market; *Chap. 11:* Ronnia Kaufman/The Stock Market; *Chap. 12:* Elizabeth Hathan; *Chap. 13:* Shoot/Picture Perfect

For Olivia Zoey, Emily Farrar, and Elizabeth Storr:
Three remarkable women who became "me, myself and I"
— all in the nick of our time.

Acknowledgments

★

First, there are my patients. They and their parents trusted me to understand and help, even when I was less certain than they that I could. It has been, and continues to be, a great privilege to learn from them the simple and complex truths of becoming fully human. They have given of their time, privacy, trust, and other treasures to help and be understood. This book simply wouldn't be, much less sing, without them.

The next family that made this book breathe was mine. My wondrous partner and wife, Marsha, whose counsel and insights into the text (and me) were peerless. Daughters Elizabeth and Emily, who first taught me what it was like to become self-made of mind and heart, and who are now helping us do the same with their little sister, Olivia. Extended family who have offered advice, priceless material, meals, patience, and their kids' stories: Dawn and Troy Pruett and offspring, the Tiltons, Mitch and Nancy Kline and children — thank you. And to friends who would be family if we could pick: the Facendas, the Israels, and the Huhns.

Friends and colleagues who have affectionately challenged, supported, loved, and nudged each other as we have tried to do the fabulous potential of the early years of life justice in our clinical work, research, teaching, and writing: Kathyrn Barnard, T. Berry Brazelton, Nancy Close, Alice Colonna, Cathy Cox, E. Kirsten Dahl, Wayne Downey, Marti Erickson, Julian Ferholt, Sarah Friedman, Martha Leonard, Alicia Lieberman, Elizabeth Loewald, Kitty Lustman-Findling, Steve Marans, Lola Nash, Barbara Nordhaus, Jeree Pawl, Sally Provence, Sam Ritvo, Ken Robson, and Joseph Saccio.

For the opportunity to work in a world-class academic environment surrounded by bright and passionate people, my deep appreciation to Donald Cohen, Irving Harris, Al Solnit, and Fred Volkmar for making the Yale Child Study Center such a yeasty and vibrant place.

Special appreciation is felt for the friendship and extraordinary competence of Bob Emde, Tiffany Field, Stephen Fleck, Nancy Hoit, Jan Johnston, Michael Lamb, Jim Leckman, Sara Sparrow, Joe Woolston, Ted Zanker, and Ed Ziegler for inspiring understanding of the harder things to see in our field.

My long association with Zero to Three: The National Center for Infants, Toddlers, and Families has been so sustaining to me, it is hard to imagine this book making much sense without the leadership, creativity, brilliance, and warm society of the remarkable staff (Carol Berman, Lynette Ciervo, Linda Eggbeer, Emily Fenichel, Haida McGovern, Matthew Melmed, and Elie Szanton), and the unparalleled members of the hardest working board of directors in the non-profit world. This field would be barren and lonely without you: Maria Chavez, Bob Harmon, Linda Gilkerson, Stan Greenspan, Megan Gunnar, Sheila Kamerman, Ron Lally, Bernie Levy, Sam Meisels, Harriet Meyer, Doddy Norton, Joy Osofsky, Arnie Sameroff, Mickey Segal, Rebecca Shahmoon Shanock, Jack Shonkoff, Bernice Weissbourd, Serena Wieder, Gordon Williamson, Harry Wright and Barry Zuckerman.

Finally, my gratitude to the hard-working and talented people at Goddard Press, who have been in this book with me from beginning and whose inspiration it was to write it — Anthony Martino, the chairman of Goddard Press and The Goddard Schools, for his generous support; Diane Lansing, Editor-in-Chief, for ably and tirelessly leading the effort; and Suzanne du Pont and Fran Ritter of the Goddard Schools, for their advice and counsel. Nancy Booth's researching and writing were critical in the early drafts. For those I have inadvertently omitted, my apologies. ★

— *Kyle Pruett, Guilford, Connecticut*

CONTENTS

★

The speed and force of growth in every facet of a child's being from 18 to 36 months. How and why this is the best of all possible times to guide a child to a lifetime of joy and accomplishment.

New findings force changes in the way we think about growth, nature, nurture, and personality. Why daily experience matters more than we thought.

Figuring out your child's and your own. How they shape a child's perception of the world and his connection to you.

The roots of autonomy, self-reliance, self-regard and the "trying (not-so-terrible) twos." The passion, thrills, and chills of exploration. The beginnings of body mastery and sensuality unplugged.

Learning memory, curiosity, intelligence: What they are and how they are measured.

Language explosions. Behavior that speaks when words fail. Saying what they mean and understanding when they can't.

When play is more than fun and becomes the work of understanding. Figuring out the real from the not-so-real.

Introduction

★

From 18 to 36 months stretches one of the most engaging and vibrant periods in your child's life. What makes you a believer? Perhaps a kiss — that first spontaneous smooch on the face guaranteed to melt a parent's heart. Or a long, shared glance that means you absolutely understand each other. Or you'll find it in your little one's joy with words and their power to communicate and comfort.

This is a time of phenomenal growth filled with promise. What happens in this short but critically important time will have a profound and lasting impact on the adult your child will become.

Your child enters this period with a freshly emerging sense of self. Over the next 18 months, that new sense of self will blossom into a clear identity. Never again are the body, mind, and heart so accepting of, and comfortable with, each other. Your child will take a great leap forward in defining the independent person he or she is and wants to be. Competence, personality and self-image — the keys to accomplishment and achievement in every aspect of living — are being shaped for a lifetime.

Clearly, the care children receive in this period matters a great deal. Maybe because parents sense this, they continually say they want and need more information on how to parent during this critical period. I see their concerns expressed over and over in national surveys, in the soaring demand for parenting books and magazines, and in the questions I hear every day.

The problem for parents is the growing gap between 1) their own bred-in-the-bone instincts to parent in a particular way, 2) what they hear blaring from the media about infant development, and 3) confidence in what they know about their role in raising their kids.

No doubt, part of this dilemma stems from the torrent of news on the fascinating findings about brain development, especially in the first three years of life. Science is now a staple of parenting magazines. Unfortunately, science coverage is a mixed blessing. Spot coverage of isolated findings cannot possibly do justice to the total body of what we know. On top of this, the media seems preoccupied with how to accelerate early learning. This has given many parents a distorted view of what's really important for their children's development into whole people who can love and learn across a lifetime.

There is a lot more happening with your young child's development than the lop-sided coverage of cognitive growth would have you believe. The physical, language, and cognitive milestones — first steps, first words, first feelings, first thoughts — just don't get to the heart of what's happening or to the point of what parents are asking about the child's emerging heart and spirit.

At the other end of the spectrum, many excellent books address the medical, physical, and safety issues of early childhood. But most skirt the development of a child's fundamental "personhood." Yet the joy of seeing and guiding the emergence of their child's total "being" is what most people look forward to when they become parents. It may be the only thing that sustains them in the dark or confused moments of the job.

The total picture emerging from our research should reassure and encourage parents. This book is designed to give you that total picture.

★

UNDERSTANDING THE BALANCE

You will learn in this book that there is a better way to understand and guide your child's development than by concentrating on early learning or waiting for the next developmental advance. You will also learn that the breadth and variety of normal growth in these years is amazing indeed. No toddler or preschooler, even an identical twin, looks or behaves exactly like any other.

We will focus on how a child's personality takes shape in these months in all of its richness and depth. We will also show you why the way you provide care is critical at this formative stage for every facet of your child's being. Not only do children grow at an unprecedented rate into very particular persons during this period, but this is when parents have the greatest influence in helping to set their child on a healthy and happy course for life. We'll show you the many tools you already have — in your child's own temperament, style, needs, and wants — to help you get your child on the right path for a lifetime.

Children are wonderfully resilient. But with parenting, as with most things, getting it right somewhere near the beginning makes life easier for everyone. If you can wonder at and understand what's happing in this extraordinary period, you'll be in great shape to guide your child's growth (and yours as a parent) and to be delighted and amazed by it along the way.

Unlike the other books on this shelf, this one reminds you to listen to the essential dialogue between development of your child's mind (learning) and heart (feeling). That is where *real* growing up happens. Supporting your child's total development through this *total* approach is the key to shaping your youngster's personhood in ways that unlock every promising thing your child brought into this world. ★

CHAPTER 1

The Importance of Being Two

The speed and force of growth in every facet of a child's being from 18 to 36 months. How and why this is the best of all possible times to guide a child to a lifetime of joy and accomplishment.

From the dawn of recorded history, parenting advice has preoccu-pied humankind. Right after agricultural and political advice, ancient rulers asked their sages what (on earth!) to do about their chil-dren. Israelites, Persians, Moguls, Asian emperors, Sultans and Roman emperors, such as Tiberius and Augustus, all sought and gave advice regarding the rearing of children to be productive, moral, smart, respect-ful, and well. The topic is never far from human thought and history, devoted as it is to the preservation of the species.

In this book, we examine toddlerhood, traditionally understood as the era that begins when a child is walking competently and gaining physical and motor autonomy. It is generally viewed as ending with toilet training and readiness for group learning — the hallmarks of the preschool era.

I've chosen to focus on these eighteen months because *they are the keystone in the archway of personality formation*. This is not simply some bridge joining two more important land masses of infancy and childhood. It is a time of life wholly unto itself, a critical period deserving to stand on its own two feet.

A WORD ABOUT WORDS

"Toddler" takes its name from the reaching of a physical milestone, where-as "preschooler" has its root meaning in reaching the preparatory phase of a social learning environment. The first just happens maturationally and the second says school is more important than being. As a clinician and developmentalist, I think these unfortunate names belittle the complexity of being such a child, let alone raising one, in this critical period of growth of personality. While the terms occasionally come in handy, I generally rely on the word "child."

Modern science has underscored the importance of this period in dramatic ways.

- ★ **Neurobiologists have captured on film the staggering growth of the brain in the first three years of life.**

- ★ **Developmental researchers have proven the remarkable effects of early care on enhancing or retarding cognitive growth and learning ability.**

- ★ **Behavioral scientists have shown how successfully children of this age can be taught to overcome temperamental difficulties, such as excessive shyness.**

The foundations of all aspects of a child's competence, personality and temperament are being set for life during this extraordinary year and a half. What parents do with and for their children at this time matters a great deal — for now and for a lifetime.

At the same time, toddlerhood is also one of the most delicious periods of human life.

When I have promising medical students with a special interest in human development as well as healing, I connive to get them in the room with an 18- to 36-month-old, just so they can experience the vitality and robust quality of the child's desire simply to be with people and find out what they are about. If that doesn't convince students to respect children in their own right and not just as diminutive adults, I counsel them out of the field.

Why? Because human beings are rarely as guilelessly or powerfully in love with simply being alive, hour by hour, as they are at 18 to 36 months. The body and mind embrace each other as equal partners in a powerful dance that neither can do alone. The sensuality of physical growth and body mastery balances with such passionate curiosity and hunger for competence that the appetite for new experiences is satisfied only with exhaustion or frustration. The good news is that parents who understand this balance and their place in maintaining and enjoying it need not fear. They'll do the right things and have a wonderful time parenting.

One of a Kind Right from Birth

Any nurse in the newborn nursery will tell you that even before they are dry, newborns exhibit different temperaments and personality traits. Some cry, some don't, some look, some move, but none is a clone of any other baby.

Yes, they are different from the start and get even more so as they grow and develop. The fascinating work by Stella Chess and Alexander Thomas in the New York Longitudinal Study, now more than 25 years old, proved beyond a doubt that children are born with unique temperamental characteristics as a result of certain genetic predispositions that account for such differences.

However, studies have also shown that it is the *interaction* of the child — whether "naturally" shy or exuberant, quiet or rambunctious, emotional or mellow — with the nurturing domain that eventually shapes the direction the inborn traits will take.

And of course as parents, the nurturing domain is largely yours.

The Way We Nurture Nature

We have come a long way from the insights of Sigmund Freud, who felt the goals of human development were to lower frustration and limit aggressive impulses. His daughter, Anna, nudged us toward a more interactive, relationship model. In her view, positive caregiver-child relationships formed the bedrock of normal, trusting human relationships. This is certainly closer to the way today's parents see their role.

No longer is it helpful to our understanding to pit nature against nurture. Healthy development begs them to cooperate. *What matters most is the way we nurture nature.* This is a major theme throughout this book.

A mountain of good research shows us how much you matter in this business of nurturing nature. A theme that we will weave into every chapter is this: *human relationships are what make our young human.* Biology and genetics alone, without the profound contribution of care and nurture in a trusting relationship, fall short again and again, as our prison populations so often attest.

Three examples:

★Jerome Kagan of Harvard University has shown compelling evidence that parental types profoundly affect the way that temperamentally shy children, in particular, turn out. He looked at babies four months of age and studied them again when they were in school. The wary and mistrustful kids whose parents over-protected them and simply accepted the shyness as a fate which they could not affect, stayed on the sidelines of their worlds and looked timid.

However, parents who supported their shy kids' smallest efforts at exploration and persistently nudged them forward in the world — encouraged them to "get in there and be a player" — had kids whose shyness eased considerably. Here, a documented genetic predisposition seen at the age of four months was significantly shaped and led in a positive direction by consistent parental behavior toward the child.

★Craig and Sharon Ramey at the University of Alabama at Birmingham have shown that even high-risk babies off to a shaky start in life aren't doomed to trouble. Early intervention with the parents of these infants, who were generally low-birth-weight and sometimes drug-exposed, and with the children themselves, produced dramatic improvements in many areas, including cognitive development and language ability.

★Kathryn Barnard of the University of Washington, whom Dr. T. Berry Brazelton has called "America's Best Nurse," has shown that even the sickest "premie," one of nature's least able humans, can be nurtured in ways that maximize the chances of full recovery in a big way. Dr. Barnard observed that the diminished responsivity of the prematurely born infant — that "nobody's home look" — is so discouraging to parents that it is hard for them to stick with the baby emotionally when so little is coming back. She teaches parents to follow up on even the smallest signals, letting the baby know that someone is home and encouraging the baby to interact. Sure enough, the infant catches on, the parent-baby dance gets going, and the baby thrives.

The common thread here is the responsiveness of infants and toddlers and their capacity to soak up and benefit from attentive, loving care. How parents nurture the nature of each child helps set the solid foundation for the growth to come.

A Question of Balance

Parents who understand this balance of nature and nurture and their place in maintaining and enjoying it need not fear. Throughout this book you will see that there are interesting reassurances in the profound new findings about genetics and the brain. We will help you *use* what's useful and ignore the rest. You will also see that the breadth and variety of normal growth in these months is amazing indeed.

In fact, when we encourage a harmony of nature and nurture, we see healthy environments *alter the architecture of the brain itself* in healthier ways. This alteration can, in turn, encourage more helpful genetic expressions and discourage others. You simply can't underestimate how much good you can do for your kids once you have this dance clear in your mind. Yes, *mind.* The brain alone is insufficient to the cause.

It's the Everyday Moment That Counts

In the above examples of parents who coaxed their toddlers out of shyness or engaged their premies into relationships or overcame their at-risk status, success flowed from changes in everyday routines. A child's being is shaped in the mold of daily life and forged hour by hour in the relationships that make up that life. Children pick up on and are deeply affected by the general atmosphere that pervades the home or the forces that shape family life on a daily basis.

And in this daily routine, the effect of what you do with and to your children is filtered through the way that you are with or are doing it to them. An "I love you" hissed through clinched teeth out of guilt after yelling at a testing 12-month-old fools no one. The extraordinary Jeree Pawl of Center for Infant-Parent Psychotherapy at the University of California-San Francisco summed this up wonderfully: *"The way you are is as important as what you do."*

Hidden in this catchy little phrase (which you will see a lot in this book) is the idea that the way you behave and feel as you go through the everyday moments of life with your young child matters as much as the things you do with or to your child. It isn't just the dressing or feeding techniques you use when caring for your child, though they, too, matter. It's the tone of the interaction that deeply affects the process.

Without including the tone of the interchange, it is very hard to understand how the child experiences you or the outside world as a whole. Without knowing the "way" of the interaction, we remain pretty deaf to what is happening between us as parent and child. It's like trying to sing a song by reciting the words alone: the melody may not be everything, but it's incredibly important.

Disciplining a child when you are out of control yourself doesn't work. It doesn't work even if you say the right words and do the right thing, because the tone is all wrong. If you are calm and clear and believe in your need and ability to keep your child safe, it will work better because the tone will be as convincing, if not more so, than the words or deeds of your response.

Getting in the Game

What we are really talking about here is the emotional content of the relationship. The "tone" is all about how we feel. Emotional growth is the underreported cornerstone of early childhood development. There are no props or toys that teach emotional growth, and the subject rarely makes headlines. But it's the emotions that drive all other types of learning. And it's through the emotions that parents can most fully connect with their children.

> ★ It's the flicker of interest from the shy child that catches the attentive parent's eye and opens a door to engagement.

> ★ It's the ability to connect at the right emotional level when your child isn't doing well that greatly increases the efficiency of your guidance.

Parents are pretty good at knowing the physical landmarks of their children's growth and development: the rolling overs, the sitting ups, the standings, the walkings, etc. That's nice, but it is hardly where the real action is in helping your child turn into a human being. Such information can be reassuring, but it clearly understates the impact on a child's overall development. From a practical standpoint, I've discovered in my decades of work with parents and families that it doesn't turn out to be very useful in the long run. It's like scoring a baseball game: the scoring keeps you interested, or at least awake, while you are waiting for the next thing to happen. But it is nothing compared to being on the field.

On the field, you *feel* what is happening, sweat, do right and wrong things, and play a part in the outcome. What is much more helpful to parents is an understanding of that feeling of "being in the game," feeling part of what will happen next, sensing what needs to occur for things to move forward. Knowing a timetable that suggests when your children will walk or talk is comforting, but it is peanuts compared to understanding how their world changes when they move through the world on their own, or actually say what they mean and get what they want without a frustrating guessing game.

The difference between *measuring* your child's growth and *understanding* it is like the difference between describing who your child is in inches and pounds and describing the child in terms of what she loves, can't stand, or couldn't live without. It's "Sarah is 34 inches tall and weighs 23 pounds," versus "Sarah loves climbing the jungle gym, hates lima beans and wants to hear *Good Night Moon* over and over every bedtime."

And then there's the part about how *your* world changes when your child reaches a new level of competence! Knowing what she is capable of feeling and communicating to you emotionally is vastly more useful because it means you know how and where to connect with her by using your own feelings.

The Emotional Foundation of Growth

Emotional development goes right to the heart of the adult that parents want their child to become — interested and adventuresome, trusting and cooperative, confident and secure, able to solve problems and enjoy life to the fullest. These are the attributes that enable people to lead fulfilling lives as caring, accomplished human beings. Parents know, and science confirms, that they must understand, nurture, shape, and guide these attributes for their children to develop their talents, achieve their potential and become productive citizens. But how to do it?

Although there is no simple answer, you will find that emotions, themselves, can be your greatest ally. Emotions provide an open channel you can use any time, anywhere to "read," connect with, and guide your child. Emotions provide the best window on the heart and spirit — happy? sad? frightened? transitional? ashamed?… They are also the most direct path to thinking and learning.

Emotional growth, and the social skills that flow from it, deal with the personhood of the child – the wants, needs, quirks, passions, interests, foibles and joys. In fact, *the really crucial milestones along the way for both you and your child are more emotional than physical.*

The goal of this book is to bring a better balance to parents' knowledge about what's really going on with their children in this amazing period of 18 to 36 months. At no other time in a child's life will parents have the same impact on shaping the adult their child will become. Here's what we now know:

★ Interest, curiosity, and a lifelong love of learning are forged on the anvil of emotional development.

★ The ability to trust, share, cooperate, and love are rooted in how the emotions are shaped.

★ Confidence, drive, and perseverence are products of emotional balance and maturity.

★ Contentment, pleasure, exuberance, and enjoyment of life depend upon the ability to feel and fully express these feelings.

★ Solving problems, resolving conflicts, restraining anger, coping with frustration, and overcoming disappointment all require the ability to feel and manage these emotions.

★ Emotions drive children to gain competence, which includes getting and giving help when it's needed.

Parents who are concerned about cognitive development may focus on early learning props and programs. But emotion and feeling, both the parents' and the child's, are what really drive learning most efficiently. Children who are in a good mood learn better. If they are interested in what they are learning and enjoying what they are doing, the neuro-chemical environment in the brain keeps their interest engaged. Memory, too, is really a chemical reaction of sorts in the brain, and the younger the child, the busier and richer the neighborhood in which that reaction takes place. Everything nearby in that brain is nosy and wants to get involved.

The emotions give you the best window to know what's going on with your child. Emotions provide the best link for you to connect with your child. And emotions are the most encompassing and powerful attributes to use to enjoy, share with, guide, teach, and eventually discipline your child.

Rich with Possibilities

Looking at the emotional context of your child's life opens up a whole new way of seeing and feeling what both of you are doing. For example, so much is involved in even the simplest game. Peekaboo can be rich with possibilities.

★ Consider this: A round of peekaboo doesn't just happen. Someone has to start it. At first, you did, of course. But why? What were you feeling when you started this intimate little game? Playful? Irritated and needing to distract yourself with a little magic? In need of some reassurance that you matter to the little guy? That you will always "be there for him" when the hands open over the eyes? That he will "always be there for you?"

★ Once it is started, then what? How long do you play? You have to read your child's response. If it's fun, you'll both keep at it. If not, at least one of you will quit. Do you still try to reconnect and save the game? Your child's reaction matters as much as yours.

This is a short list of what could be at work here, but there is always something. And the emotional "something" matters a great deal, because that is how the event gets remembered. The way it *feels* to be together and how you both *feel* in that togetherness matters every bit as much as the child's neuro-muscular ability to open and close his eyes at will, smile, make eye contact, blow spittle bubbles, or giggle.

This will only make sense to you if you understand that your child can feel many things long before he can tell you in words, and that understanding emotional milestones benefits both of you enormously.

What's Ahead

Of course, I know parents live in the real world where mothers of very young children work, where fathers often feel on the sidelines, and time is a most precious commodity. I know mothers and fathers are occasionally tempted to overparent to compensate for these erosions in parental esteem.

This book will help you sort out these issues as I keep reminding you of this maxim as well: Development is pushed and pulled along by the child's motivation to be competent, your desire to give the child the best life you can, and by your understanding that the really crucial milestones along the way for both of you are more emotional than physical.

Each chapter will explore particular facets of your child's growth in this era and their impact on your relationship with your child. Suggestions are tied to the real and practical, as well as the evidence-driven. By the end of this book, you should feel closer to, and more in touch with, your child and yourself as a parent. You'll be a more comfortable expert in your own right, as well, because you'll know that you are the only *real* expert in the life of your child…ever. ★

CHAPTER 2

The Young Child's Brain and Mind

New findings force changes in the way we think about growth, nature, nurture, and personality. Why daily experience matters more than we thought.

By the time your child is 18 months old, there will be no doubt in your mind that she has her own — *mind,* that is. Every time she chooses carrots over peas, laughs during a game of peekaboo, toddles toward the dog, or coyly says, "No," she is expressing a unique mind — a self, a burgeoning personality — that is hers alone. And during the next 18 months, she will move from an awareness that she is separate from others to a sense of her own identity. She will change from a dependent baby to an independent child. You will see the change, and you will *feel* it even more. It's a great adventure!

Of course the physical growth, motor competencies and the explosion of language during this period are the most apparent. But in fact, it is the emotional growth, the establishment of self-identity, that matters more to the adult your child will become.

To understand this growth, we first need to turn to some of the extraordinary findings about development in children this age. To start, I'd like to share some exciting new information about the brain and how it becomes a mind. The brain and its early growth set the stage for virtually every other facet of development. In recent years we have come to understand a lot about what it can do and how it grows. There is also much we still haven't got a clue about.

What is particularly noteworthy is something talented parents, teachers, and clinicians have suspected for years: *physical brain growth and the development of the mind are spurred on by pleasurable environments and loving caretakers.* The architecture of the brain can actually be altered by experience.

Here's how:

The Brain

Of the more than 100,000 genes that make us unique, more than one-third of them are dedicated to carrying information related to the development, care, and feeding of the brain. They serve as blueprints for how the brain grows before birth and will be shaped thereafter. Brain cells, called neurons, are formed very early in pregnancy and start migrating to their designated homeland almost immediately.

A baby is born with a full complement of neurons — about 100 billion. But the neurons are not well connected at birth. Links between cells, called synapses, form at a rapid-fire pace in the early years, reaching their peak of about 1,000 trillion by the time a child is just three years old.

This synaptic formation begins soon after birth, as the environment around the child, especially the human (relational) environment, begins to "switch on" certain developmental processes in the brain.

The evidence for this is dramatic, thanks in part to a remarkable new advance in brain imaging technology known as positron-emission tomography (PET). Dr. Harry Chugani, a pediatric neurobiologist at Wayne State University in Detroit, has given us dramatic visual evidence of the phenomenal growth of the brain during a child's early years.

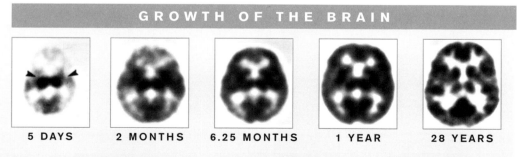

GROWTH OF THE BRAIN

| 5 DAYS | 2 MONTHS | 6.25 MONTHS | 1 YEAR | 28 YEARS |

Source: Harry T. Chugani, M.D., Children's Hospital of Michigan/Wayne State University

Furthermore, the astonishing plasticity of the brain — its capacity to change and compensate — in the early years is also well-documented. This resilience is dramatically demonstrated in cases of children with a variety of disorders. For example, in children with life-threatening, intractable epilepsy who have had an entire hemisphere of their brain removed, the remaining hemisphere gains in both mass and function, and vital neural pathways are re-established, allowing substantial recovery of lost functions.

Experience as a Catalyst

Researchers have shown that early childhood experiences powerfully impact the young brain's growth. The child's nurturing environment actually affects the way the neural circuits of the brain are wired.

The parts of the brain having to do with emotions and attachment, particularly the limbic system and the brain stem, start getting connected to the thinking parts of the brain (the cortex) shortly before birth. Some of these connections run through the parts of the brain that deal with body control mechanisms, such as eating, heartbeat, and breathing. This wiring arrangement predates the birth of the baby, but it doesn't get well organized until it has to help first the baby, then the infant, then the 18- to 36-month-old, interact with, and figure out how to make sense of, the surrounding world. In other words, *emotions and physiology get connected very early. What happens in one area affects the others.*

We know from extensive research that the more interesting the information this system has to carry, the more sophisticated the system becomes, and the more elaborate the brain circuitry becomes. *What seems to drive mental development furthest is the richness of the connections between the learning and feeling centers of the brain.*

This richness occurs in conjunction with, and probably because of, the specialized growth and differentiation in the brain that occurs during this 18- to 36-month period. PET scans of the brains of Romanian orphans, who received food and shelter but no emotional attention, show far less development than those of children from emotionally supportive environments. The differences are a powerful testament to the importance and effect of love and attention on the brain's development.

The temporal lobes (which are responsible for receiving input from the senses and regulating emotions) in the brains of children from healthy environments are rich with activity. Those of attention-starved children are hauntingly quiet.

Moreover, research shows that the effect of high-quality care goes far beyond early cognitive learning. Social skills, responsiveness, emotional expression and control are all interconnected with rapid brain development. Equally important, research shows that children learn best in the context of an affectionate everyday life, especially with a caring adult.

Use It or Lose It

After the furious pace of synaptic growth in the first three years, the process starts to reverse. The cranial cavity runs out of growing room. Unneeded and unused synapses begin to be shed, or pruned. This process continues until adolescence. By then the number of synapses is reduced by half.

How do you "use" or preserve an infant's or young child's brain cells and connections? Same as for an adult: stimulation. The more a synapse is used, the more it will be strengthened and likely to last.

It is environments rich in pleasurable experience, especially when matched to the child's appetite for such experience, that encourage durable synaptic proliferation. Enriched environments encourage connections. The more these connections are used, the more efficient they become, and, therefore, are preserved. Meanwhile, their less-used counterparts don't survive the pruning process. A classic case of "use it or lose it."

This information is at the root of all the excitement about early learning and the surge of growth during the first three years of life. Unfortunately, it is also at the root of a lot of confusion and misunderstanding of what this information means.

The seductions of the new neuroscience findings are hard for us to fathom. It is so exciting and comforting to think that we could actually have some control over what happens to us and our children, and we want so much to believe that we have discovered the one true path to doing so.

Yet, time and time again, we learn in life and in science that it is hardly ever that simple. Everything from air bags to Vitamin C, tobacco to vaccinations, are not the wonderful, no-strings-attached improvements of the human condition which they first appeared to be. So even though we want to believe in Mozart, flash cards, and infant swimming lessons, we will see that success in life rarely has to do with such frenetic, narrowly focused early programs.

Nowhere is that better understood than in programs such as Head Start, where success is high even though resources are scarce. In the decades of experience Head Start has had with hundreds of thousands of young children, the program has made only modest use of "enrichment" curricula. In fact, their own list of predictors for success in life emphasizes problem-solving skills, social competence and emotional security — not second languages or manipulative or spatial skills.

The most valuable enrichment activities are those of everyday life when children have opportunities to discover at their own pace and in their own way, especially when they are encouraged by caring and responsive adults.

The Active Mind

Although a frenetic push to accelerated learning misses the mark, there is an important message for parents from the neuroscientists: the brain and the mind do not thrive when they are repeatedly idle for long periods of time.

It is easy to see this in our grown-up selves. As adults, our minds are constantly on the go. Whether we are solving problems of the cosmos or gazing out the window and daydreaming, our minds are active whenever we are awake and a lot of the time when we sleep. We typically alternate our mental activity among three states: 1) actively concentrating on a task or problem; 2) receiving and reacting to external input (such as a movie); 3) thinking-to-ourselves time (such as when we gaze out the window and daydream).

The balance among these three allows each to relieve and fuel the others. If you take away one, the others get strained. Too much concentrated effort at work, and most people start to burn out. Too much input from the outside, and most people start to tune out. Too much internally directed "personal" time, and most people get antsy.

It is in such imbalanced circumstances that we hear of the extraordinary accounts by POWs, especially those in solitary confinement. Part of their battle for survival is the fight to keep their minds active. They recite poetry they memorized in tenth grade, compose mental letters to loved ones, reenact favorite TV shows, play word games, and anything else they can think of. They draw on a lifetime store of memories for stimulation.

The point is, adults need input from the outside to keep them mentally alert and healthy. The same is true for young children, albeit in a slightly different way.

★A two-year-old's "lifetime store of memories" is pretty sparse — far too little to occupy his mind when he is idle. A toddler can keep himself busy up to a point with toys and games. But he requires the attention, encouragement, and support of others to make his activity as meaningful and beneficial as possible. So do adults, but a toddler's threshold of need for others is *much* lower than an adult's.

★Without sufficient activity with other people, the toddler's brain and mind don't stay as active as they should, and *the brain probably won't get properly wired in the first place.* This is the sad plight of those Romanian orphans with the under-developed brains. It is also the plight of children from homes or childcare settings where they are severely neglected.

The first three years of life are when the brain powers up for a lifetime. If this process is shorted, the result can be developmental delays and, possibly, irreversible harm.

For most parents, the primary application of this lesson concerns out-of-home childcare. Such care *must* provide adequate, responsive, one-on-one attention by caregivers to each child every day. A childcare center that meets only the physical needs of its children can be actively harmful. Caregiver-child interaction is one of the primary requirements parents must look for when choosing a childcare center or preschool.

Overdoing a Good Thing

The flip side of inadequate care is overstimulation. With all the current focus on accelerated learning, parents may be tempted to do too much of a good thing, jettisoning playful games and enjoyable family events in favor of boring early learning programs. As with adults, too much input from the outside can cause children to tune out.

Children at this age have a fierce drive to learn, and they are thrilled with their new discoveries. This is a wonderful time to strengthen the foundation for a child's lifelong love of learning. The key is to do it in a way that respects and responds to each child's interests, pace, and temperament, and not to some external need to keep up with the Joneses or their kids.

One well-documented trait of children who do well in school is that they love to learn. Activities that build love of learning are money in the bank for a child's educational success. You don't want to squelch that drive to learn by substituting joyless, skill-pushing memory activities for real exploration, discovery, and learning.

Follow the Cues

So what do you do? Follow your child's cues. Other than fatigue, cues are all emotional. Children show interest or disinterest, curiosity or frustration, boredom or enjoyment, impatience or pleasure, anger or delight. Pay attention to your child's moods and heed his cues. Sometimes parents find this hard to do. If you are engaged in some activity you think is really worthwhile, it's easy to push the envelope until your child seriously wants out. There is no gain in this. Much better to move on to something else or just give things a rest when your child begins to show disinterest or fatigue. You know all the signs. No one is as expert as you at reading your child.

At this age, the best learning is filled with a blend of wonder, giggles, excitement, interest, concentration, a touch of manageable frustration, concerted effort, and laughter — all signs of the most positive emotional states. Lessons learned and achievements mastered in these states are gilt-edged in three ways:

- ★ **The child learns something new.**
- ★ **The child learns more about how to learn.**
- ★ **The child enjoys learning.**

KEY FINDINGS ON BRAIN DEVELOPMENT*

★ Human development hinges on the interplay between nature and nurture.

★ Early care has a decisive and long-lasting impact on how people develop, their ability to learn, and their capacity to regulate their own emotions.

★ The human brain has a remarkable capacity to change, but timing is crucial.

★ There are times when negative experiences or the absence of appropriate stimulation are more likely to have serious and sustained effects.

★ Evidence amassed over the last decade points to the wisdom and efficacy of prevention and early intervention.

RETHINKING THE BRAIN*

Old Thinking...	New Thinking...
How a brain develops depends on the genes you are born with.	How a brain develops hinges on a complex interplay between the genes you're born with and the experiences you have.
The experiences you have before age three have a limited impact on later development.	Early experiences have a decisive impact on the architecture of the brain, and on the nature and extent of adult capacities.
A secure relationship with a primary caregiver creates a favorable context for early development and learning. Brain development is linear: the brain's capacity to learn and change grows steadily as an infant progresses toward adulthood.	Early interactions don't just create a context, they directly affect the way the brain is "wired." Brain development is non-linear: there are prime times for acquiring different kinds of knowledge and skills.
A toddler's brain is much less active than the brain of a college student.	By the time children reach age three, their brains are twice as active as those of adults. Activity levels drop during adolescence.

*Reprinted with permission from the Families and Work Institute report, *Rethinking the Brain,* 1997.

The Young One's Mind

An indisputable body of research clearly shows that daily experience shapes development in our young children in ways we older, slower-growing beings can hardly fathom. Once we begin to move away from thinking "brain" to thinking "mind," we leave the laboratory and enter the real world. The 18- to 36-month-old mind is where the brain meets experience. Yes, we've already learned that experience shapes the eventual architecture of the brain, but this fact doesn't get us very far unless we say, "So what? Where is the child in all this?"

She is there, in her mind, at the intersection of tissue, thinking, and feeling. Taken together, this intersection forms the mind. As parents, you don't know what's on a child's brain, but you know what is on her mind. You know this by what she tells you or shows you through her behavior.

At the Beach

My wife Marsha was holding our 20-month-old niece, Madison, under her tiny arms, dangling Madison's feet close to the edge of the beach where morning waves were inching up, bringing the incoming tide. Calm but excited, they were completely caught up in an experiment. This was Madison's first time at the ocean, and the little researcher was letting her foot pass in and out of the surface of the water. She watched transfixed as her foot nearly disappeared, then reappeared, each time she let it pass into the water. Marsha suspended Madison's 20 pounds silently but safely, allowing Madison to decide when she wanted to go lower and get closer to this dance floor of light, sand, and water.

After three or four minutes, Madison signaled with a little wiggle that she wanted more, and Marsha obliged with a reassuring commentary on what Madison seemed to want to do. They exchanged glances – a quick eye-to-eye "check in" – and down Madison went, bearing her own weight in six inches of Atlantic Ocean.

Holding tight to Marsha's hands for balance, she started lifting her feet, first one, then the other. She shifted her weight and stepped in and out of the water, apparently marveling at how her foot could not only pass through the surface of the water, but that she could still see it under the water, as well. She also seemed intrigued that although her foot appeared sightly misshapen under water, it reappeared whole with each step out. Peals of giggles and laughter erupted.

In this scene, we have two brains, two bodies, and two personalities engaged in an exploration of an everyday moment. And what a moment! First and foremost, emotional development is going on — the kind that drives all other types of learning. Was Madison being taught anything here? Was she learning? Was she enjoying herself? Of course. How were my wife and I sure she was learning and having a good time? By how Madison's behavior made us *feel*.

Our feelings enabled us to know what was happening in Madison's mind. Note that we are not talking about "brain," but "mind." And how about Marsha? Does it matter that she was enjoying herself and that both of them were getting a kick out of what was happening? Very much.

What Is "Learning?" How Do We Do It?

The brain-mind connection naturally brings up the topic of learning. "Early learning" is a hot subject for many parents who want to give their kids a head start. But just what do we mean by "learning?" For many adults, "learning" means "memorizing." We all slogged through the learn-by-rote routines to memorize a host of facts during our school days, and we recall the boredom and unfortunate transience of it all.

Nonetheless, our personal histories of memorizing, plus the push by the makers of early learning toys and gadgets, have kept the focus on this limited learning-is-memorizing concept. Hence flash cards for infants, etc.

Actually, learning is much more complicated. Memory is a component, to be sure. But right in the mix are experience, brain chemicals, sensations and, as we saw with Madison at the beach, emotions. Each of these is affected by the others, as well as by physical health and condition, and the context in which the "lesson" occurs.

Neurons are connected to one another by axons, which transmit infor-mation, and dendrites, which receive information. Information is passed between cells by electrical impulses. These impulses trigger the release of brain chemicals, called neurotransmitters. There are 40 some different neurotrans-mitters, each with its own job. Some excite activity, others impede it. Some work quickly, others gradually. You've probably heard of some of them, such as serotonin, epinephrine, and dopamine.

Chain Reactions and Ripple Effects

With all these components, learning is not an isolated event. Instead, *learning is a highly integrated set of actions and reactions among components,* rather like the ripples on a pond that intersect and transform one another when pebbles are tossed in the water. Moreover, these reactions can be viewed at increasingly complex levels.

★ First, we can look at just the neurochemical changes in brain cells that are brought on by a single event.

★ Second, we can look at the wider interaction of sensation, perception, and cognition as an event occurs. In this case we would look for changes in many areas of the brain as well as in the child's behavior.

★ Finally, we can look at the regular patterns of interactions of sensation, perception, and cognition that are the stuff of everyday life. These are the familiar occurrences at meal and bath times, when petting the dog, greeting a parent just home from work, reading a story, or playing with a favorite toy. These events, too, are forged in external events and inter-nal changes in the brain. Over time *these patterns begin to transform behavior into personality.*

If a child is happy and interested in what he is doing and discovering, he will probably repeat a new action over and over. His initial action triggers a neural response. If the action pleases him, the neurochemical changes may prompt him to repeat the action. This repetition builds and strengthens the synapses required to perform and remember the action (yes, practice makes perfect!). The neurotransmitters released in the process help him feel good about his newly-acquired discovery or skill and encourage him to discover and learn even more. When a caring adult cheers his success, the ripples and reactions really multiply!

In all of this, emotions are central. Yes, interest is an emotion. So is boredom. When we are interested and enjoying what we do, we learn faster and want to learn more. No doubt you can remember some really arcane stuff because it was taught by your favorite teacher who made the subject come alive.

The Mind-Heart Connection

Emotion and learning are so connected in these early years that children are most delighted when they learn with a person to whom they are emotionally related. This is where the third level of chain reactions and ripples comes into play. Memory centers are connected repeatedly and redundantly to emotional processing centers in the brain. This makes it possible to file new information and retrieve it more easily when pleasurable human associations accompany the filing of that information, whether it's a new food, a new word, or a new moment at the beach.

As noted earlier in the chapter, we now know that brain "wiring" not only makes such a moment possible for a child, but that the wiring itself is *responding* to the moment at precisely the same time. Now we'll begin to think about how wiring works itself into becoming a mind and how we can help things along.

Transactional Analysis

Arnold Sameroff of the University of Michigan has shown that it is not simply the interaction between parent and child that helps a child be mindful of their interaction. Rather it is the *transaction* between the two that drives or discourages the child's development. This is an iterative process at a more complex level than a simple interaction. This is the third level — the personality/relationship level described above. Dr. Sameroff says it is not enough simply to see things as happening *between* child and parent. What really matters is how each action affects the next, and how that affects the next, and the next, and so forth.

As a parent develops patterns with a child to comfort him, to pick him up, read to him, tuck him in, say no or get mad, the child synthesizes the smell, touch, sound, and feel of these moments of everyday life. He takes these details and stores them preconsciously and counts on them to be the same next time, like the smell of coffee in the morning to a coffee drinker, or of freshly-mown hay to a country kid. Children *count* on the meaning and value of details and feel comforted by the very first sign that things are going to unfold and feel a particular way between the two of you.

Soon the back-and-forth feedback about how you are coming across to each other — the moods you are both in, whether one of you is tired or bored — becomes a transaction of a relationship, not simply an interaction between two people. "One mind can only know itself in relation to another" seems to be the bottom line.

Here again, we see that the way you are is as important as what you do. That particular way becomes an emotional image that is stored in the child's mind for future reference. These images are priceless down the road when non-parental childcare is underway, and the child needs to feel loved and safe, to feel Mom or Dad. Like a soothing corner of quilt, the stored image calms and organizes the child's emotions.

Transactions as the Basis for Attachment

The patterns described above are the basis for the attachments people form with one another. Pleasurable, attuned, and consistent human relationships are secure attachments, and, as such, are *mind-enhancing forces*. Madison's relationship to Marsha helped set the stage for her discovery at the beach, and Madison's enjoyment of that discovery strengthened her ties to Marsha.

Attachment research has matured in recent years and now has interesting things to say to us, especially through the work of Alan Sroufe of the University of Minnesota. Although the way you are is as important as what you do, Dr. Sroufe reminds us that *what* you do is also important, and it's more important than what you say to your child, especially when that child is very young. It is the predictive link between the particular patterns of your interaction with each other that shows up down the road in patterns of self-control, or the lack of same.

Dr. Sroufe studies infants and then follows them through childhood and adolescence. Kids with secure attachments to their caregivers — where they experience predictable transactions together in the daily grind that are attuned, pleasurable, and trustworthy — are characterized later by more effective self-control and an ability to regulate their emotions. When such security is lacking, so will self-control be lacking down the road.

Attachment is built over time in the course of everyday transactions when children learn that they can rely on their parents for affection and encouragement and that they can trust their parents to come to their aid. All of this needs to happen in a way that respects and responds to each child's needs and temperament. Over time, the security of attachment actually frees a child to venture more fully into the world to explore and learn. *A healthy childhood is a dance between the magnetic attraction to trusted parents and the powerful pull of the outside world.*

WHAT DOES IT MEAN?

A word on behalf of all parents who think about the well-being of their little ones. To be thinking *at all* about what a child's behavior might mean is a sign of a deep, healthy connection with the mind of the child. Whether a decision you make concerning an issue is ultimately "right" or "wrong," thinking about your child's behavior is a good thing to be doing, because it signals and reinforces how involved you are with your child's experience.

Although we'll take a longer look later at how children's and parents' styles fit, it's a good idea to think together about how kids and parents get into each others' heads when children are racing full speed ahead at becoming themselves.

Images and Expectations

As if the reactions and ripples weren't complex enough, we also need to add the adult mind into the equation of a child's development. A child's mind may be raw material, but a parent's mind is another matter. Each of us comes into our role as parent filled with hopes and dreams of what we want to give our children, what we think is important, and mistakes we want to avoid. It's a big load, one worth continually reappraising. Parents' hopes and expectations play a huge role in how they respond to their child. These responses, in turn, get added to the mix that forms the environment in which a child grows. Let's look at an example.

The Would-Be Tomboy

Sara was working full-time at convincing her mother that she was not quite what her mother thought she should be. Her mother had grown up in a chaotic but loving home and consequently wanted a behaved and quiet daughter who appreciated the sacrifices she was making for her. Sara's mother played soothing New Age music whenever changing or bathing Sara, kept the lights soft in the house, and worked overtime at keeping her and her husband's voices "below a dull roar." Even the dog was selected for her mellow, "ladylike" temperament.

Meanwhile, Sara was sitting up at five months, was walking at 10 months, and was rolling a ball back and forth from the time she could avoid slumping over. Climbing on furniture was her favorite goat-getter. In fact, whenever anyone in her home, family or friends, was on a knee for any reason — adjusting a video, or oiling a hinge — Sara was scaling them like a technical rock climber from the time she was 16 months old. It wasn't just her strength and balance skills that were impressive, it was the diligence and determination she brought to these enthusiasms. She clearly loved her body and everything it could do. Behaving "like a lady" was not high on her list of priorities.

Consequently, there was some trouble brewing here. I visited the home to get a good picture of what the parents were concerned about. As I hung out, I saw a healthy and boisterous little girl, cute and sturdy, who might have been called a Tomboy, before the advent of political correctness. I spent my time watching her with her parents and tried to help them see that their daughter really needed them to see who she was. I worked to get them to start thinking differently about her and concentrate on what she loved to do and be, rather than focusing on what they needed from her. The struggling against "type" was exhausting the parents and confusing their daughter. Although Sara would have been called securely-attached according to Allen Sroufe's definitions, she was straining at her traces and needed her parents to give her her head, lest she begin to feel less secure in who she needed to be.

Although the 18- to 36-month-old can still seem very young, neuro-development and personality formation are such that *children this age are actually approaching middle age in terms of becoming who they are really meant to be.* That is why these early years are so important in figuring out who you and your child are to one another and getting comfortable going down the same road together.

Many Minds Shape a Child's Mind

All this adds up to the conclusion that we cannot talk about the mind of an 18- to 36-month-old without automatically evoking the other minds around it. We have come to know and understand that it is *how we nurture nature that matters more than the effect of either force alone.* It is the interaction between emotional, social, and cognitive development that matters so profoundly.

Parents worry about these early critical periods of mind and brain development because it reminds them that there are limits to certain windows of opportunity. Yes, growth is remarkably plastic and flexible. Just watch the two-year-old whose leg comes out of a cast that has kept her from walking for months. She will spend every waking moment of the ensuing days trying out her freshly-knitted bones. Usually children this age show not so much as a hitch within weeks of cast removal.

One window that does not remain open indefinitely is the capacity to develop trust. Infants raised in harrowing conditions, such as in Romanian orphanages or the American institutions before the reforms in the 1960s, grew up trusting only themselves to scavenge for food and relationships, having little hope that anyone was out there who would ever feel crazy about them. A brutal life in a brutal world.

Meaning in Everyday Moments

By the age of 36 months, most children have experienced remarkable growth in the integration of emotional, physical, and interpersonal development. And while the complexity of this accomplishment is enormous, sometimes a child's ability to carry out an apparently simple act can tell us a great deal about how well that child is doing.

The elegant example of the "Toddler's Kiss," offered by my wonderful mentor, Dr. Sally Provence, describes just such an act. This is a wondrous achievement — a complex blend of physical skill, learning, imitation, interaction, and emotion. First presented when she received an award from the American Academy of Pediatrics, Dr. Provence introduced this poignant observation, which I share to help you appreciate what we really mean by the development of mind, and not simply brain.

Of all a child's new accomplishments, none is more precious than the first time a child puckers up and kisses a parent's face. Dr. Provence shows how this simple act tell us so much. She notes that this is a normal accomplishment by around 18 months:

"The young child's kiss has the advantage of being an ordinary event — one which can be observed directly or which parents can usually answer when framed as a question. One might start by asking such questions as 'Is he/she an affectionate child?' 'How does he show affection?' Then, more specifically, 'Does he give you a kiss?' 'Does he really pucker or just put his mouth against your cheek?'"[1]

If a child isn't kissing by age two, Dr. Provence notes, the cause could be a neurological dysfunction, lack of affection by caregivers, or a personality problem. In any event, we should certainly ask, "Why?"

The point is, everyday events are filled with meaning. The complex sets of reactions and ripple effects in the life of an 18- to 36-month-old are rich with signs of what's going on and what is needed. It is in these signs, and the emotions conveyed in and through them, that parents can most fully connect with, understand, delight in, and guide their children. This is the true wonder of the brain and mind. ★

---

[1]From "Remarks on Receiving the C. Anderson Aldrich Award," reproduced by permission of *Pediatrics, Vol.* 59, pages 388–389, Copyright 1977.

CHAPTER 3

Temperament and Style

*Figuring out your child's and your own. How they shape
a child's perception of the world and his connection to you.*

Temperament is the style of interaction that children use to influence the world around them. Taken as a whole, it is the simplest way of talking about the emotional attributes of personality. Is your child shy or outgoing? Quiet or chatty? Daring or cautious? Timid or boisterous, or somewhere in between? Does he adapt easily to change or prefer a "let's-keep-things-as-they-are" approach? By the time your child is 18 months old, you probably have a pretty good sense of his dominant behavioral style.

The common final expression of *temperament* — filtered through the cheesecloth of *nurture* — is your child's behavior. Having a sense of your child's style lets us know how he is doing, what he needs, and whether you and he are getting through to one another. Also, it is important for parents to acknowledge their child's temperament if they wish to establish the secure attachment that is so critical to his sense of security and well-being.

Infants seem to arrive in the world equipped with unique ways of responding to their own sensations and physical processes. The journey from 18 to 36 months sees them move from self-awareness to self-assurance and finally toward self-identity. During these months, you will probably notice that some of your child's temperamental traits seem to settle in, maybe even intensify, while others will soften or even vanish.

Because there is so much uncertainty and misinformation about the origins of a child's temperament and how much influence parents have over it, I have condensed the current scientific thinking into five basic principles:

1. **Parents don't cause their child's temperament.**

2. **Temperament is not fixed at birth.**

3. **What looks like a trait in the beginning may be the interplay among many factors.**

4. **All behavior has at least some meaning.**

5. **Parenting profoundly shapes how a child turns out.**

These principles are vitally important. Moreover, they are undisputed in the realms of credible behavioral science and medicine. These principles should reassure every parent because they open so many doors to the constructive role that parents can play in the lives of their children.

Our largely Western philosophy of development includes a strong belief that what happens in childhood determines your fate. If you are happy as a child, everything will be all right. Michael Lewis, director of the Institute for the Study of Child Development in New Jersey and author of *Altering Fate,* finds this belief silly. Dr. Lewis generously estimates that only one-tenth of a child's inborn temperament survives into adulthood, while experience shapes and changes 90 percent of a child's personality traits. This chapter is about how that 90 percent is, and can be, molded by good parenting.

The Variety of Style

The infinite variety of children's personalities is a continuing delight and astonishment to parents and to those of us privileged to work with children on a daily basis. It is adapting to this variety that makes parenting more art than science.

Temperaments and behavioral tendencies of the 18- to 36-month old are neither good nor bad. They are simply raw material at this point. However, some combinations of behavior and predispositions are more challenging than others for parents.

At one end of the spectrum are the happy, easygoing, flexible kids — the ones who star in TV commercials. These children settled into predictable patterns of daily life soon after birth, cried little, smiled lots, and were well matched to their parents' styles right from the get-go. God bless them all — every one.

At the other extreme are children with behavioral predispositions which, if left unchecked, could blossom into trouble later on. Sometimes these tendencies occur alongside, or even as a result of, a physiological condition. Either way, their impact on personality development can be profound.

Then, of course, there is everything in between.

Detailed discussions of serious disorders and their treatment is outside the scope of this book. Fortunately, such problems affect a small percentage of children and families. However, I will touch on the most common behavioral patterns, because the way they are best handled offers guidance on how to work with normal children who have even mild tendencies that could profit from modification.

Another reason for touching on these issues is that 18- to 36-month-olds are especially receptive to parental guidance and encouragement. The brain is still powering up at a fantastic rate, with connections and patterns very much open to parental influence. Then, too, kids this age are highly imitative and eager to please the lead players in their lives.

In short, now is as good as it gets to encourage and foster the behavior patterns that will stand your child in good stead for a lifetime. Far easier to rechannel overly rambunctious tendencies in a two-year-old than to halt full-blown aggression in a rebellious teen.

Most of the encouragement and nurturing that guide a child at this age are common sense. However, if you are concerned about anything, I encourage you to get a second opinion and, if it looks beneficial, outside help or counsel. We don't have all the answers. Far from it. But there is a great deal that we have learned about how to get through to and support our little ones who need a helping hand.

Now let's take a look at how a child's temperament is guided and shaped during these important months.

1. PARENTS DON'T CAUSE THEIR CHILD'S TEMPERAMENT.

Parents come to realize that children seem born with predispositions of temperament. Earlier I observed that nurses swear dispositions appear full-blown in the delivery room, and that is true for some children. This is important for parents to understand, especially if they have a particularly fussy or sensitive baby.

Parents need to be reassured that a difficult temperament in a young child isn't the parents' fault. Nor is your child willfully being irritating or impossible. At 18 months, a child has not developed Machiavellian schemes to manipulate parents and others.

Temperamental styles of children are beyond their control early in life. Nineteen-month-olds usually don't wake up crying to spite their parents. A child is also unlikely to hide behind her mother at a preschool because she is trying to get people's attention. There is no reason to blame these very young ones for behavior they cannot control. There is also no reason to ascribe darker motives to such behavior when the child's cognitive development isn't up to the task of even having such a motive yet.

Temperament only describes *how* a child reacts, not *why* she reacts a particular way. Remembering that these behavioral styles are part of the child's "nature" helps us to sympathize with the child's experience. This, in turn, helps us respond constructively to unwelcome behavior. Comforting rather than scolding a child who balks at separations works better because our response fits the child's needs. And if we preserve this shy child's self-esteem, she may, in fact, be a bit bolder next time.

2. TEMPERAMENT IS NOT FIXED AT BIRTH.

While temperament is not anyone's doing, neither is it cast in stone. For centuries scientists have debated whether temperament, once set, changes. Sound research and years of clinical observations clearly show that temperament is not "fate." Here, too, *what matters is how we nurture nature.* There is plenty of evidence to back this up.

What we do with and through temperament — both our own and our children's — is what building character is all about. This is one of the greatest gifts of parenthood. It is also one of the biggest responsibilities. Strengths can be nurtured and shaped. Weaknesses can be lessened or even channeled into constructive traits.

Treating Excessive Shyness

As noted earlier, Jerome Kagan of Harvard University believes that a tendency toward wariness and shyness versus outgoing sociability is genetically programmed. However, Dr. Kagan's important research has shown us how parents can mold the way a shy or timid child perceives the world. Some parenting styles increase a child's fearfulness or cautiousness. Other styles promote curiosity and exploratory behavior.

Dr. Kagan started by looking at babies four months old. He then studied them again after they entered school. Kids whose parents supported their reluctance, made repeated excuses for them, protected and held them back, were, in fact, timid and painfully shy. Parents who supported their kids' slightest inclination to "jump in and try it" even when the kids were reluctant to "get back in there" had children whose shyness was considerably reduced and who coped better in most social situations.

For the latter group of children, what had started off as a genetic predisposition toward timidity had been reshaped and softened by parental behavior. It is probable that this change is not limited to observed behavioral difference, but is neurobiochemically altered as well. The neurological pathways that are the cable system of such behavior do change over time.

The Aggressive Child

Further grist for this mill comes from the important work of John Gottman of the University of Washington, whose follow-up studies of four-year-olds show that aggressive kids can become less impulsive, depending upon how their parents handle them. In his work, he makes a point of having parents

DIFFERENT TEMPERAMENT, DIFFERENT WORLD VIEW

Research also teaches us how a child's temperament can powerfully shape his perception of the world. The child who hangs back "sees" a smaller world than the child who presses forward. He also knows fewer people, has fewer experiences outside his small world, encounters less diversity and, over time, expects less of a world that is perceived as worrisomely intrusive. Intimacy and introverted forms of creativity and comfort from parents can help a child with such a temperament to build trust.

The rambunctious glad-hander, however, makes things happen around her, including more accidents and mistakes. However, such a child also creates excitement and interaction of all kinds. She knows more people and places, and this knowledge and experience gives her the perception that the world is a big oyster. In the long run, this in itself may bring more pleasure and joy than the few intimate, long-lasting relationships that sustain her quieter counterpart.

connect with their children emotionally as well as developmentally. Consequently, his approach is in synch with the theme of this book.

Even though the children he studies are older than the ones we are considering, his findings are consistent with the positive results parents have when they connect with their children at a feeling level. Here is a summary of Dr. Gottman's approach to behavior trouble:

- ★ First, he encourages parents to connect and validate a child's emotional state. For example: "I know you are excited, or upset, or disappointed..."

- ★ Second, he instructs parents on how to help their child verbalize what she is feeling. For example: "But tell me how it felt when..."

- ★ Third, he has parents involve the child in coming up with a solution. For example: "What should we do now to work this out?"

Over time, this kind of "emotional coaching" increased the social competence of the children Dr. Gottman studied when he re-evaluated them at age eight. Parents usually had to learn this coaching skill from scratch. They often were surprised that it worked. Once they mastered the skill, they felt increasingly competent in managing their kids' behavior. Children whose parents could not — or would not — learn emotional coaching did not show the increased social competencies.

Although Dr. Gottman's work is a good example of a thoughtful intervention on behalf of families who are off to a shaky start, I continue to be inspired by how dedicated and effective the vast majority of parents are in raising their children. This is a cardinal principle I teach my students, one that prevents us from being arrogant or judgmental — most parents are doing the best they can, and that is plenty for most kids.

Yes, there is a small percentage of deeply disturbed parents who seem to need to destroy their children's promise or even their lives. But their numbers are minuscule compared to the majority who struggle against exhaustion, sweeping uncertainties, and the limitations of parenthood to do their best for their children.

I continue to be moved by regular folks who connect wonderfully with their kids, even when it is uncertain that they can do so when we first meet.

The Biochemistry of Temperament

An exciting new area of research is focusing on how the genetic contribution to temperament/behavior actually works. Unlike genetic traits, such as eye color, which are immutable, the genetic infrastructure of behavior is more plastic. New findings are giving us some fascinating clues as to how this works.

For example, a certain DNA sequence on a particular gene named D4DR has come to be associated with the ways our bodies make use of the powerful brain chemical, dopamine. Dopamine is one of 40 some neurotransmitters that regulate how the brain receives, stores, and transmits signals to other parts of the brain and the rest of the body. Dopamine squirts into the tiny gap between nerve cells whenever a message is to be sent from one cell to another. It acts like a chemical wiring system throughout the brain.

The plot thickened when behavioral geneticists found a link between thrill- and novelty-seeking behavior and the way dopamine is used or metabolized. Other brain chemicals and neurotransmitters are being investigated to see if and how they may act as genetic mediators of certain behavioral and personality characteristics. Some of these include:

★**The role of serotonin, a mood-enhancing neurotransmitter, in avoiding stress and harm. Low or insufficient levels seem to be associated with increased aggressiveness.**

★**The role of dopamine in increasing aggression.**

★**The role of norepinephrine, another neurotransmitter, in stabilizing patterns of positive feeling and pleasure. Such patterns are obviously reinforced by important caregivers, but get hormonally mediated by norepinephrine. Yet, like dopamine, high levels of this chemical seem to cause increases in aggression.**

Clinical observation of infants and the study of brain chemistry suggest that children are born with certain tendencies of temperament. But once more I caution: It is far too easy to confuse genetic "contribution" with genetic "determinism." As I have described throughout this chapter, the evidence is overwhelming that predispositions can be modified, sometimes dramatically. The subtle, endless transactions between the care-giving environment and the child are constantly molding that genetic clay. The child with an insatiable appetite for thrills and chills can be raised as a daredevil survivalist in one household, and as a creative, reflective seeker of novel ideas and interactions in another.

There is abundant research in the many ways a young child's emotional experiences, especially those in relation to the consistent caregiver, shape how the brain develops. This development goes on to shape behavior. The process is a continuing back-and-forth, cause-and-effect evolution of brain, mind, thought, and behavior. Emotion-regulating transactions with the central caregivers shape the brain's interconnecting circuits and pathways to become enduring patterns of behavior — for good or ill. Good, well-tuned interactions help the young child balance excitement with inhibition, leading to reliable and dependable self-control.

3. WHAT LOOKS LIKE A TRAIT IN THE BEGINNING MAY BE THE INTER-PLAY AMONG MANY FACTORS.

While it is clear that certain temperamental tendencies can be modified by parental behavior and approach, even "assigning" genetic predispositions to kids can be a tricky affair. Twenty-five years of following the development of some kids I met early in my practice as a clinician makes me say "not so fast."

For example, we know from our friends the behaviorists that children can condition us — and we them — from the early months of life by rewarding and punishing in incredibly subtle and half-conscious ways. If a child feels he can reliably get his needs met, even for negative attention, with predictable behaviors, he will remember those trigger points. Exactly *when* those memories become part and parcel of influencing temperament, I am not clever enough to tell.

What does the caregiver love and reinforce about this particular behavior? What does the caregiver detest and discourage? Does the child prefer auditory over visual stimuli? In other words, is she more a listener than a watcher? Does she have to be looking at you for her "ears to work?" All senses are not created equal in all children.

A given child's physical condition can certainly play a part in our perception of temperament. An emotionally confident 18-month-old with poor muscle tone might seem shy or wary, when he's actually just unsteady on his pins.

The Non-Smiler

Tommy had been born with a neuromuscular weakness in some of his facial muscles because of an unfortunate birth trauma. He taught me a great deal about how early vulnerabilities can be made worse or better by a world that does, or does not, understand. His problem initially looked like a temperamental one, but he taught us we were wrong.

By 28 months old, Tommy didn't smile much — in fact, hardly ever. His mother was older, and he would be her only child because her husband had died in an accident during her third trimester. Despite these troubles, Tommy and his mother had gotten off to a great start with the help of extended family and stable economic resources. But the trouble had started before I met him at the one-year checkup. At that time, Tommy's mother said she couldn't get him to smile anymore. I asked her to show me what she did to try to get him to smile. She sang a soft, sweet song, and all Tommy did was look solemnly into her eyes. She also told me he was having trouble keeping food in his mouth, and we observed that, too. Eventually, we made the diagnosis of a slight facial palsy. But that was hardly the whole the story.

Tommy's mom had worked night and day for months to get him to smile after he was "supposed to start" smiling at around three months. It was very important to her self-regard as a mother that she make him smile, at her in particular. Eventually, she found herself trying less hard because her non-smiling boy seemed to be rejecting, or at the very least, not responding to her. This was very painful to her because she felt "very unimportant to him," and had "kind of given up" back when he was around 18 months old.

As we began to work with Tommy, her brother came for an extended visit. He was a very animated, "fun-loving, even rambunctious" salesman who had twin girls, but who had "...always wanted a boy. He adored Tommy and spent night and day with us for three weeks and got Tommy to smile!" Tommy's smile, once rekindled, was easier to evoke, and, as his uncle said, "Tommy doesn't make it easy, but it's worth the effort." Even his mother was now able to "turn it on," and it "meant the world" to her.

This is a clear example of how a small biological problem can become a big emotional one if we don't fully understand its impact on the child-parent transactional dance. It wasn't simply that Tommy's physical disorder had gone undetected. Part of the problem was that his mother had become discouraged and started to disconnect from her son.

If Tommy's uncle hadn't arrived to discover that Tommy actually could smile, albeit with difficulty, what at first looked like a socially-inhibited infant could very easily have become a socially-inhibited school-age child. It wasn't that

Tommy didn't love his sweet mother enough. The neuromuscular problem in his facial muscles made it hard for him to smile. Tommy's mother had wearied of supplying the cues which indicated her connection to him. Cheerful bombast from Tommy's uncle succeeded where subtlety and misunderstanding had failed. Sometimes you just need to do a lot of work.

Parents of so-called hyperactive children know how much work can be involved in helping a child cope with this less-than ideal behavioral style early in life. Both of these conditions result from a combination of temperamental and physiological factors.

The Hyperactive Child

The hyperactive child is another level beyond the high-energy child. Besides boundless activity, the hyperactive child is characterized by impulsive behavior and volatile emotions. This condition affects mostly boys, and it is present at birth. The problem is neurological, with some evidence pointing to an imbalance in brain chemicals.

The upshot is that the hyperactive child typically does not have the ability to tune out unwanted or useless input. Instead, he receives any and every sensory input at full volume. This skill of tuning out part of one's sensory environment normally starts developing early in infancy. Without it, a child has little ability to focus on what's at hand instead of the competing attraction — barking dog, TV, flushing toilet, kitchen aroma, stomach gas, etc. He is captive to every incoming sensation, and has little control over his reaction.

The key for parents is to reduce the sensory and information overload as much as possible so they can work with the child at his own pace and watch for the earliest cues that he has had enough. Encouragement and celebration at each success are essential to the mix.

Given such support, overactive children can learn to manage their behavior and do fine. But it does require a clear understanding by parents as to what the problem is, their patience and persistence, and close attention to the child's cues.

Again: Nature Versus Nurture

By this point I hope you appreciate, perhaps more than before, how crucial your role is in shaping the person your child will grow up to be. It has a profound and lasting impact on every aspect of a child's being, from learning and intelligence to curiosity and confidence, from disposition and outlook on life to perseverance and accomplishment.

Does this mean we have all the answers? Not by a long shot. There is no "paint by the numbers" formula for parents that guarantees success in raising a child. For one thing, "success" means different things to different people — thank heavens! We human beings are so complex, as are the factors that shape us, that no two people react the same way to events or environments, even when those events or environments look virtually identical.

When It Goes Wrong

Most parents do a terrific job, and their children turn out wonderfully. Yet, within the human family there are individuals who simply baffle us. Most of us know of loving families who have great kids, except for one child who just can't seem to get on the right track. The most extreme cases make the news, as in the seemingly inexplicable tragedies of youth crime and violence.

So the debate continues: if the families were "good," were these children just born "bad?" The answer is no. Genes contribute to, but do not cause behavior, any more than starting your car one morning caused the parking ticket you got later that day. Children clearly exhibit widely varying temperaments and predispositions. And, as we've noted earlier, some of these are easier to manage than others. Also some are closer to parents' temperaments and, therefore, parents can understand and guide them more easily.

That said, parenting counts. Parents who cherish the individuality of their children are in the best position to draw out all that is wonderful in each child. And attentive parents are best able to spot difficulties that need extra attention, possibly from professionals. Who better than you to help your little one get the help you clearly see she needs?

The important message is this: parents should not view inexplicably troubled children as a sign that parenting doesn't matter. It does — especially in these early years when the foundations of personality and emotional health are built. Parents who decide to "wash their hands" of a troublesome young child, declaring that the child must have been "genetically fated" to be difficult, are doing that child a tragic disservice.

While we do not know the neurobiological mechanism by which parental behavior shapes child development, or why some seemingly physically healthy children may be beset with troubles, to relegate nurturing to the cheap seats behind genetic determinism flies in the face of science and defies common sense.

Lest we get too far away from the real world, the best we can do is establish islands of consistency with our kids and ask that other caregivers follow our rules as best they can. This raises the important question of the caregiver's temperament and how it fits, or doesn't fit, with the child's. Can librarians successfully (even happily) raise sky divers and vice versa? Of course. And if you don't forget your sense of humor, it can be a fascinating journey. (And to those librarians who are also sky divers, I'm counting on your sense of humor here, as well!)

Many parents probably remember a friend from high school or a roommate from college whose style and temperament were wildly divergent from their own. Yet friendship grew, and the very differences that may have startled them at first became an invitation to a brave new buffet of friends, sports, values, music, culture, etc. The child with the "different" temperament can take a parent on a similarly enriching excursion.

Understanding this helps us avoid the mistake of thinking of a "bad fit" between parent and child. There is no value judgment to be made here, any more than for eye color or the placement of a cowlick. Matches are either easy or complex, not good or bad. True enough, some fits require more adjustment and energy than others, but raising a clone would be devastatingly (and prob-

CAN LIBRARIANS SUCCESSFULLY RAISE SKY DIVERS – AND VICE VERSA?

How's the Fit?

Test yourself with the following questions. As you go through them, think about how your child would answer them.

- ★ Are you action-oriented or do you prefer quieter, less physical activities?

- ★ Do you like routines, or is variety the spice of life for you?

- ★ How do you react to new people or new activities? Do you jump right in or do you need time to feel comfortable?

- ★ How do you react to change? Do you go with the flow or do you resist change?

- ★ What kind and level of physical activity do you like?

- ★ Are there certain kinds of textures or touch that you find pleasing? Displeasing?

- ★ Do you prefer firm hugs or a more gentle touch?

- ★ Do you like being physically close to others or do you like your own space?

- ★ Are you sensitive to certain smells, sounds, or light?

- ★ Are you intense or laid back?

- ★ Are you easily distracted or is it easy for you to concentrate?

- ★ Are your moods fairly stable, or do they vary throughout the day? Are some times of the day better for you than others? If so, which times?

- ★ Are you generally a happy person? Generally irritable?

- ★ Do you get frustrated easily?

You probably can think of other questions as well. All of the questions, however, can help you to pinpoint areas where you and your child are "in synch" and where you're not. Then you can find ways to accommodate and learn from one another.

ably dangerously) boring to parent and child — no humor, no teasing, no teaching, and no learning.

What we see in research over and over is that parents who accept, value, and react appropriately to each child's individuality have the happiest outcomes. A few common cases illustrate the point:

Consistent Response

Responding to a child's needs *invariably* works better than ignoring them. Parents who consistently and promptly respond to the determined cries (and not every whimper) of a colicky baby or sensitive child build the trust and attachment that typically help bring the child out of the "fussy" stage sooner rather than later. Such attentive parents also are better able to identify and eliminate "triggers" that cause upsets in the first place. Research has debunked the notion that ignoring a child's needs "builds character." It doesn't. Ignoring the needs of children at this age simply teaches them that no one will come to their aid, and that they are on their own — not a useful lesson for a toddler.

Great Expectations

Parents who can put their own ambitions or expectations for their child aside and encourage their child's natural interests not only have happier kids, they enjoy parenting a lot more. This gets back to our discussion of librarians and sky divers.

Reflections on the Past

Parents must also recognize and manage their own fears or preconceptions about human behavior so they don't misunderstand their child's actions. For example, an adult who grew up with a demanding or abusive parent may wrongly interpret a child's negativism or rambunctiousness, which are normal for children this age. Parents who are a product of such unfortunate circumstances must be candid about how those experiences could color the way they view a child's behavior. Then they must adjust their thinking and actions accordingly.

A Parent, Not a Friend

Some parents want to be their child's "friend." Stella Chess's and Alexander Thomas's New York Longitudinal Study of the development of temperament over time taught us that a parent who looks for — and tries to raise — a buddy is frustrated every time. The drive for autonomy and separateness varies from child to child, but it serves the child and us well in the long run. If you, as parent, need a buddy, turn to a spouse or other friends, not your kids. They need a parent much more than you need a friend.

4. ALL BEHAVIOR HAS AT LEAST SOME MEANING.

As I noted earlier, behavior is the final common pathway of temperament filtered through nurture. However we understand any particular child's behavior on any given day, I want to state a belief held by most of us in the young child mental health field: All behavior has at least some meaning.

Specific behavior may mean different things to different people, but it means something. The two-year-old's hands-on-hips "harrumph," the deep-eyed look of the infant, the three-year-old's taunting of the family pet, the father running his fingers through his sleeping daughter's hair — it all means plenty.

We may not always get it right, but we must appreciate that behavior and style are the products of many things: chronological age, personality and temperament, ethnic and cultural roots, traditions and hopes of family and community, developmental age, and, of course, experience. It is a river that has drained many mountains to come to look the way it does to our eyes.

5. PARENTING PROFOUNDLY SHAPES HOW A CHILD TURNS OUT.

This is the crux of this chapter. If parenting is powerful enough to help children overcome serious behavioral difficulties — as the research I have cited shows — its impact *for any child* cannot be in doubt. Your parenting at this stage will greatly affect the way your child's temperament is shaped for the long term.

This period is the final run up to getting the brain fully wired, which is virtually complete by age three. As the brain is still very plastic at this stage, so are the mind and temperament. This time is rich with potential — greater than you will ever encounter again — to encourage positive traits and tendencies and to correct or modify those that could pose a challenge to healthy growth and a happy childhood.

The tools for encouragement or correction are the same: reading and responding to a child's cues. These cues are all emotional — the flicker of interest in the shy child, the wrinkled forehead of the bored child, the delight in the child who's just mastered a new skill, and the pout of the child whose exploration is suddenly curtailed.

None of this is to say that your life must revolve around your child's every whim. But it does say that even very young children have a broad range of interests, needs, and preferences that can and should be reasonably accommodated. Your child's emotional cues at this age let you know what's happening, and they give you the keys to unlock the best possibilities. ★

CHAPTER 4

"Me Do!"

*The roots of autonomy, self-reliance, self-regard, and
the "trying (not-so-terrible) twos." The passion, thrills, and chills of exploration.
The beginnings of body mastery and sensuality unplugged.*

In the fourth century A.D., the Roman Emperor Julian requested that his personal physician, Oribasius, write a treatise on all that the Roman world knew about medicine. It took 70 volumes, and Book V was devoted to kids and their well-being.

In Chapter xiv, Oribasius complained that parents often attended their horses better than their children and sounded like a good behavioral pediatrician: "Infants who have just been weaned [in Rome it was about now], should be permitted to live at their ease and enjoy themselves: they should be habituated to repose of the mind and exercise in which little deceptions and gaiety play a part…" He even presaged the wise observations of modern child development specialists regarding the importance of attitude in nurturing: "Relaxation and a joyous spirit contribute much to digestion and favorable nutrition…"

The self — the *ME* — of the young child emerges in this 18-month era with such force that it feels more like a geologic event than a stage in development. After months and months of figuring out what is me and *not* me in the world, children are so anxious to put this new understanding to a test that we, as parents, often feel that all we can do is direct traffic.

Wrong. Even though our little guys seem to have no interest in trap doors and blind alleys, we know all too well that dragons lurk everywhere. And we must be determined to aid and protect our little ones in their quest for self-identity.

In this chapter, I'll discuss the child's tremendous push for autonomy and separation from home base, how to keep a child feeling secure in her wanderings and explorations, and the skills involved in more remote kinds of parenting. In all of this, it's important to remember that although this push looks exhaustingly physical, it is, in fact the emotional growth that matters most.

During this 18-month period, your child does not go about anything without emotionally feeling everything and exploring everything physically through the senses. It was, after all, in studying this period of development that Freud coined the term "pleasure principle." No kidding! "If it feels good, do it, and do it NOW" is the manifesto of these 18 months.

This philosophy invades the kitchen, the bathroom, and the bedroom. The child pursues it because she has learned to connect how the world feels to her at a sensory level with what she's trying to get across regarding her needs or feelings to the important people in her world. And she now understands that when she is plugged into that world, it responds reliably to what she does or needs.

The Push for Autonomy

The drive to autonomy encompasses the body, mind, and emotions. Your child will be enthralled to discover and exert this newfound control.

Body: Your child rapidly gains appreciation of his body as the wonderful contraption that gets him to all the new and interesting places and things he wants to find out about. Expect him to explore himself along with everything else ("Wow! What's this?" and "Ooh, that feels *good*!"). Add to this his maturing awareness that he is a separate being — not an extension of you — and you can practically hear him marvel that his body is *"mine, all mine*!"

Mind: The discovery of independence goes hand in hand with the independent spirit — wanting to do what she wants, do it her way, and do it by herself. This is a crucial period in the development of self-esteem and respect for others.

Emotions: This period sees the beginnings of emotional control. Yet learning and discovery pull at the toddler, pitting the thrill of success against the agony of frustration. Through it all, the emotional underpinnings of learning will be strengthened or weakened. Either way, the lesson will have long-term implications for the drive to discover and learn.

In terms of behavior, children start off this period with a new but immature interest in controlling themselves. Their limit-testing behavior is more about who they are apart from their parents, as opposed to seeing who is boss. They are learning to handle some of the simple routines of everyday life like forks and spoons, and choosing an occasional favorite item of clothing. They even can begin to share a little, but usually not for long.

Emotionally, they begin this era fluctuating between growing independence and wanting to be a baby again. They can be very loving to the people around, patting and kissing faces or stroking hair (mimicking the affections they appreciate). They can mirror parental feelings with amazing accuracy.

Eighteen months later, they will be able to control most of their own behavior, and their baby-longings will be less frequent. They will be able to tell their parents a lot about their world, be much more able to share, and be more respectful and caring of others. Pretending and sharing will be possible on most good days, even in your absence. Throwing and kicking balls around, and getting dressed by themselves will probably be reliable skills as well. In short, it is a breathless 18 months of growth in the evolution of a person.

Home Base Versus the Outside World

As children grow into their second 18 months of life, they are faced with a very difficult duality: the need to explore versus the need for a secure base. This is what gives the era the name of the not-so-terrible, but oh-so-trying twos.

Starting around 18 months, the child begins a new dance between his uncharted independence, and the familiar secure base of his loving relationship with his parents. It can be cute at first, with clinging and hugging one moment, pushing and darting away the next. It often catches a first-time parent by surprise — suddenly the little guy is off by himself around the corner, when last week he melted down if you picked up the phone for a moment. After a loving reunion, you put him down, he starts to play comfortably, and it starts all over again. After the next reunion, he won't let you out of touching distance, much less his sight, shadowing every move in your space! The child is searching for just the right distance that will allow him to be part of your physical and emotional space while keeping his own little courtyard inviolate.

This is what makes these few months such an important proving ground for developing the skills to cope with the frustrating challenges and dilemmas of adult life. More forcefully than during any other era, these months bring kids face-to-face with two powerful yet contradictory impulses. First is the intense longing to feel safe and secure in the predictable domain of familiar and intimate relationships. Second is the thrilling exhilaration of unfettered and uninhibited exploration free of the obligation to look back over the shoulder to see who is disappearing in the distance.

You see this push-pull in your child's physical maneuverings. But the psychological dimension is where the real action takes place. What feels like a safe proximity or distance is a product of the child's increasingly capable thought process, not the result of where he is sitting or standing at any given moment. It is common for children at this stage to have some level of separation anxiety. At this point, attentive parenting pays real dividends when you can pick up on what level of distance he really wants and when you can accommodate his need for space and exploration while still keeping him safe.

Toddlers embrace this duality with great passion, and the balance between intimacy and exploration has implications that cast long shadows over the developmental eras that follow. Our unique equation of this balance, together with our temperament and experience, creates an individual style from which we rarely stray for the rest of our lives.

Jason's behavior in the following example is a good demonstration of how this duality looks. Parents who are alert for cues will not only recognize Jason's expression of autonomy, but his need to "check in" with his secure base.

By the Pool

At 21 months, Jason wasn't talking much yet, but boy, did he have a lot to say! Of the 400-plus words he would say a day, "Me do!" accounted for 75 percent of them. On this particular day, he'd finally gotten down to the pool at his grandparent's apartment complex, the place he'd been angling to get to since he'd awakened from his nap. Naked but for his diaper, he was thrilled to be padding around the edge of the pool of bright blue water, getting close enough to the edge every 10 paces or so to satisfy his curiosity and titillate the vigilant grownups.

He was a good walker, but his stubbornness and independence worried them all. He was not inclined to listen to his parent's prohibitions once he was in an exploring mood. As he lost interest in the water and wandered off to investigate the new landscaping, the mulch pricked the bottom of his feet, and he began to wail. His mother started to go to his aid, but his father yelled, "He'll be fine, let's just watch him a minute."

In fact, Jason sat down on the cement and quieted as he picked the offending bark from between his toes. More mad then hurt, he pushed himself back up on his feet, muttering "me do" as he toddled back toward the pool. A single glance toward his parents was all he needed before he set off behind a big smile to join the other kids hanging around the water slide.

Jason, in this one example, could be seen as a pretty self-contained child. His own desire to explore got him into a bit of trouble which he managed himself with only a glance at his parents. Had his mother intervened, we don't know what might have happened. But he attended to his own trouble, and narrated his success with a casual, self-directed "me do." His smile may have been relief, even pride — we don't know. But at the very least, it was a marker of internal pleasure at doing what he did, or just in being who he is.

My niece, at 20 months, had a different repertoire of behavior prior to exploration. Before she would head off to investigate the den, the dog, or the lawn, she would find her mother or father, touch them very gently on the leg — with or without eye contact — and then strike out on her own. There was no real change in her facial expression, but her gait would quicken with excitement after the touch, as though she had received some extra amperage to stow in her batteries.

Through all this, trust in the home base and parental support is essential to the child's ability to learn. Without that trust, learning through exploration of the outside world gets short-circuited by anxiety. Children must be able to trust that parents will keep them from harm — that if some new experiment is dangerous, Mom or Dad will jump to the rescue. They also need to know that parents will respect and help them to overcome their fears and frustrations and the outbursts these emotions may bring. A few basic guidelines for this process are:

★ **When your toddler has trouble controlling herself, give a few (two or three at the most) clear, simple, and consistent rules. Follow with eye contact or remove her from the scene, if necessary. Note that grabbing a child and muscling her around generally angers an independence-bound toddler.**

★ **When your child is testing limits, be sparse in your usage of "no." The more you use it, the less your child will believe, or even hear, you. Use distraction or diversion, and save the big "no" for issues of personal safety and danger.**

★ **Give a frustrated child time to communicate with you. Children under duress don't always understand cause and effect, or even why you are so upset.**

The Body of Knowledge

Much of a toddler's activity is devoted to exploring the body, mostly theirs but quite often yours, as well. Depending on the number of siblings and other group care experiences, most children love to explore their bodies' abilities and orifices during this era, with a peak somewhere between 22 and 26 months. Depending on their temperament and yours, this may be more public or private, but it will happen, nonetheless.

The body is the child's means of access to the outside world. No wonder she wants to figure out how it looks and feels, and how and why it does what it does. On top of that, she's only just discovered that her body is hers alone — not an extension of you. All the more reason to plumb its wonders! Expect lots of close examination, poking and touching every inch, staring with fascination in the mirror, and trying to figure out what this being is all about. Discovering genitals and the pleasure they can give are high on the list of important toddler moments. Running around in the buff is a source of sheer delight for children this age whose natural exhibitionism is in high gear.

When your toddler shows such obvious joy and pleasure in his own wonderful little body, it is very important to let him sense or see your pleasure in that wonderfulness. That incredible unity of his sensuality, pride, and fascination with every inch of the world never reaches this harmony again, so let your enthusiasm for that achievement be very obvious.

Smiling, laughing, hugging, and admiring make your enthusiasm believable. This doesn't mean you call the local news station with every body-display. Follow the dictates of your own culture and family values regarding childhood nudity, but this is *not* the time to introduce shame about the body. Your child is just getting to know this body as his own and not yours.

When self-exploration occurs in a situation that is less appropriate than you would like, don't make a fuss. It's usually easy to distract a child with a toy. Or you can remind your child that you know that such touching feels good, but it should be done at home.

Gender confusion is normal at this stage, but passes as the child's understanding grows. The best advice is to answer questions as your child asks, but don't over-explain.

Words and Meaning

One of the great ways children of this age learn is through language. The very act of naming items — learning and using the words that properly describe people, things, attributes, and feelings — is central to discovery. Among other things, words provide a way to organize the onslaught of information children are absorbing and processing.

Although language will be discussed more thoroughly in Chapter 6, this is a good place to note that naming is not limited to things, but includes experiences, too. In the following example, Tamara's words refer not to an object, but to something more complex.

"Bye-Bye?"

Tamara is the first-born daughter of two 23-year-olds, married only a year and a half. She is their pride and joy, but money is tight, and they are working split shifts of the same job and not seeing much of each other. They hate this arrangement, but consider it short-term in order to afford better housing. Needless to say, they do not relish their good-byes.

Tamara is struggling, at 23 months, to sort out the comings and goings, not to mention the feelings connected with them. She usually has a calm and predictable temperament, but can become tyrannical and "melt down" around comings and goings if not well-prepared for them. In fact, when her cousins or uncles are getting ready to leave after a visit, she will anticipate their departure with a soft, but insistent "bye-bye?" said with an inquiring tone at the end of the phrase. It's as though she is asking, "Do you have to go?"

What is so striking is the emotional richness of Tamara's query, not just its uncanny accuracy. It appears this is a thing worth figuring out for her. Maybe if she can be the boss of the comings and goings, they won't hurt or confuse quite so much. Language has great power to comfort.

Will and Desire

As the toddler comes to grips with the profound discovery that her body is hers alone, so she begins to discover that she has a will that is also hers alone.

A child's desire to establish her will as a matter of substance is very strong in most children at this particular time. Daily dances of stubborn disagreement, followed by resolution, sweet reconciliation, followed by stubborn disagreement, etc. become bedrock under future emotional maturity. What makes it so important is that it establishes the child as "not-the-mother," yet she is no less worthy of understanding and appreciation. Arguments and disagreements with loved ones can come and go, be angry and loving, and everyone, as well as the relationship, survives just fine.

By around 18 months, many children have bridged feeling and emotion to the idea of intentional action. This opens up the wonderful new world of social interaction. The child begins to understand that his behavior has an effect on the important people in his world. And even without words, he begins to elaborate on pre-verbal communication — gestures, facial expressions, squeals, raspberries, etc. He can delight or frustrate, tease or please, surprise or reject. Some actions get him held and adored, while others get him spurned. Even before language develops, he is learning how the rules of the external physical world work through everyday interactions and moments with his caregivers.

For example, even before they are two years old, children can exhibit surprisingly sophisticated behavior in relationship to exerting their own will while still being mindful of the will of others.

The Soft Touch

By 21 months, Madison had developed a powerful technique for preventing upset in her parents when she was about to push the limits of what they would accept. Impish behavior, perhaps even impish feelings, often were preceded by a preemptive smile and prolonged eye-contact. She needed to extract a promise of good connection before she toddled off to wreak havoc.

She would come up to her mom or dad, lean up against them or a piece of nearby furniture, make a small noise or grunt, smile a huge, beguiling smile, and proceed on her way to torment the dog or crawl up a forbidden stair. It was not that she was willfully provoking her parents. It did seem, however, that she could make a connection between prepared upset parents and surprised upset parents. She could be quite separate from them in such experiences without being worrisomely separated from them.

Through such experiences, children build an inner world of feeling and emotional strength, weaknesses and soft spots, flexibilities and vulnerabilities. It is the particular mixture of these strengths paired with vulnerabilities that determine a person's ability to cope as they grow older. It is usually the soft spots and vulnerabilities that worry parents more, though many children do fine sorting them out as they mature.

For example, the child whose feelings are hurt very easily when he is bullied probably learns over time to socialize mostly in smaller groups with trusted friends, avoiding large group encounters that tend to favor loudmouths and bullies. Parents can be very helpful in steering kids in directions that help them cope with their fears:

- ★ Toddlers who fear the dark can carry the flashlight, or turn on the switch while being held in their parent's arms.

- ★ Toddlers who fear separations can cope better when given the chance to be the leaver rather than the "left behind." A spouse or older sibling can take a hand and suggest something really cool to do and leave the parent for a change, giving the child a sense of mastery over painful partings.

- ★ The toddler who is afraid of "go down drain" in kitchen or bathtub, can play on a stool beside the adult at the sink and experiment with little and big things going down the drain, the point being to show them in a secure, playful setting they are way too big to fit.

- ★ In general, any activity that allows the child the opportunity to be the actor or perpetrator of a solution instead of a victim is a good, coping enhancer.

Comings and Goings

You're about to leave for a long-awaited night on the town. As you head for the door your young one dissolves into wails that could wake the dead, and your evening is off to a warm and wonderful start. Not all children experience separation anxiety, but it is pretty common to this period.

The good news is that you can minimize distress if you understand where your child is coming from and if you plan and manage the event. An abrupt departure, being left in unfamiliar surroundings or with strangers, or extended separations can cause extra stress for a child. In each case, the child is struggling with uncertainties about the security of home base.

The key is to be sensitive to your child's normal level of anxiety and take into account any new ingredients that are going to be thrown into the mix on a given departure, such as a new babysitter or a new teacher at preschool. A more detailed list of strategies to minimize upsets related to childcare centers will be found on pages 167 – 8 in Chapter 9.

New Sides of the Social Self

The new awareness of self opens some fascinating new dimensions of the toddler mind. The discovery of "me" versus "not-me" leads to such tantalizing concepts as "mine" versus "not-mine" as well as the individuality of other people. So we start dealing with such issues as possession and sharing. We also get to a new level of awareness about who and what other people are, especially other children.

Toys and other objects are important extensions of a young child. They can be played with and learned from, and they can be used to achieve other goals — a pail and shovel are a big help in building a sand castle. But possession or ownership has more than practical applications. It becomes another means by which a child exerts independence and autonomy.

This carries over into play with other children. For children who are not in a childcare setting on a regular basis, territorial disputes are more the rule than the exception in playgroups of kids this age. That is why it usually works better to have a mix of ages rather than a group of age clones.

TODDLER'S PROPERTY LAWS

Whoever coined the phrase, "Possession is nine-tenths of the law," must have been the parent of a toddler. Right after "no," the next most frequent word from many toddlers is "mine." This is a natural, and often amusing, component of the child's new sense of self. The following humorous take on the issue has been around, in various forms, for years. It certainly reflects universal experience.

Toddler's Property Laws

1. If I like it, it's mine.

2. If it might be mine, it's mine.

3. If it's in my hand, it's mine.

4. If I can take it from you, it's mine.

5. If I had it before, it's mine.

6. If I'm making something, all the parts are mine.

7. If it's mine, it must never appear to be yours in any way.

8. If it looks like mine, it's mine.

9. If I think it's mine, it's mine.

Children at the younger end of this era do not know how to take turns or share, so do yourself a favor and don't expect much. However, you can help them ease into the delights of group play by supplying several copies of the favored toy, and staying close at hand to "catch them being good," and guiding them when they are not. Redirection and/or distraction works better than a barrage of no's.

Children in group childcare are a bit ahead of the curve on playing with other children for two reasons. First, they are accustomed to being around other children a lot, so group play is the norm, not the exception. Second, they have likely had a lot of guidance from caregivers in the basics of play with their peers. Experience counts.

The Link Between Emotion and Learning

A child's growing social skills with others — both children and adults — greatly expands the world of learning opportunities. As the brain and nervous system grow, children become capable of more complex emotional responses.

★ **The toddler takes his mother's hand and pulls her to the toy box because he remembers where it is and *feels* competent; he knows they will have fun and that makes him *feel* good; he knows she will make it fun, and he knows he will *feel* good making her happy as they have fun together.**

★ **He wants her help getting a snack because it will taste good, and he will *feel* good, and then he can go off and do something else because he knows that, too, will *feel* good.**

None of this would make any sense without feeling and emotion, regardless of how good his memory or coordination are. It has to feel good to happen in this way. Intentional behavior and thinking are ordered and organized more by emotion and feeling than by intelligence.

It is fascinating to watch children this age work on the problem of "what to feel when." Just as they experiment with new physical skills or new words, they also have the interest and ability to explore the effect of emotion on themselves and the world around them.

To Cry or Not to Cry, That Is the Question

Jason, the pool-side wanderer described earlier, had returned from his explorations of the water slide, having been splashed a few too many times by his older cousins, and told — also a few too many times — to stay away from the edge of the pool. He crawled up on his grandmother's lap, uncertain what to feel.

He was glad to be in a safe haven, but he missed the good times with the guys. As he looked longingly at the water slide crew, his face began to wrinkle up into a cry, then it got stuck in a grimace. He then tried to push through a smile at his grandfather who had empathetically noticed his confusion. Still flummoxed, Jason pursed his lips as if to close off any utterance, got flushed, nearly cried, uttered a whimper, then simply howled. After a few deep breaths, he was apparently relieved, pushed off grandma's lap, and went to pet the dog.

We can but guess at what Jason was truly feeling. Of course, this whole scene would be more easily managed and understood as he became more verbal. But if we believe that the face is the window to emotion, we can assume that he was exploring a pretty broad range of feelings. What we need to remember from his efforts is that we, too, are experimenting with understanding what our 18- to 36-month-olds are working to convey to us about their inner worlds, and it takes some time and work.

Building a Pattern of Success

Jason's mixed emotions are the product of his young mind coming to grips with the complexities of his expanding world. Positive and negative emotions are central to his growth. Like all of us, Jason needs to learn to express his positive emotions and to manage his negative ones. Key to that management is the ability to solve problems, complete tasks, and accomplish what he wants.

Children need to learn to succeed and to be willing to try new things and tackle new challenges if they are to feel competent. Children who experience too much frustration and failure inevitably begin to try less and less. The emotional discomfort is too hard, and their best tactic becomes avoidance.

But an essential part of learning to succeed is coping with frustration and sticking with the project until it works. This is another area where parents can give their kids a wonderful leg up. Once again, the key is to follow the child's emotional cues.

In teaching your child to succeed, you want to manage frustration, not eliminate it. It's fine for your child to have to work at solving a puzzle or putting on her boots. It may take her a while, and your patience is essential. Keep letting her work the problem until you see signs that frustration is beginning to overwhelm the process. (Those emotional cues, again.) If this happens, give her a helping hand, but let her finish on her own.

She needs to feel that burst of pleasure that comes with a win. This is how she commits her new discovery to memory. It's also how she learns that effort + success = pleasure. Your praise of her accomplishment makes that pleasure even greater, and the whole process gets amplified.

It's important to remember that children need to earn their success for it to feel the way it should. It's great for you to grab that last puzzle piece that scooted under the sofa and place it where your child can see it. But if you take the piece and finish the puzzle, you just ruined *his* project! For a success to count, it needs to be your child's success, not yours. And, yes, don't forget to praise *his* success.

The Long Journey to Full Autonomy

I'd like to emphasize that the search for autonomy only begins in this era in earnest, but that it does not come to fruition until the end of adolescence, which this phase can occasionally resemble. It is, after all, only practice for the totally separate, independent existence as a young adult. At least in our culture.

Unlike infants, the 18- to 36-month-old has a good chance at regulating, even modulating his more intense feelings most of the time. But meltdowns happen whenever coping skills are not up to a specific task or level of exhaustion. That is when competent and supportive parenting matters a lot. Helping a decompensating child get hold of himself at this age usually involves physical, verbal, and emotional techniques used together. Lap time is a favorite way to regroup, but it depends on the problem.

In the end, the "Me Do" era sees children moving closer to self-control and self-regulation of feeling states. Both are based on growing self-determination and intention. Despite frustrations, they remain committed to the "me" and strive toward the "do" whenever possible. While parents are fellow travelers in this journey and sources of great support, they also can become road-blocks, and frustrations can arise in their child anew. This is what the art of parenting is all about — learning from the mistakes and going on to the next move. It's how you and your child grow together and as individuals. ★

WAKEFUL NIGHTS

Growing up is heady stuff for kids. So sleep problems are not uncommon. If your child routinely has trouble getting to sleep or wakes up at night and needs comforting, his developmental achievements give you some important new tools to work with at this age. Klaus Minde and his colleagues have developed a program that helps parents understand the source of the problem and apply practical solutions.

Dr. Minde reminds parents of the importance of routine in the daily life of a child. At an age when children are learning so much so fast, predictability and regularity in the timing and location of meals, bathing, and bedtimes is soothing and comforting. In today's environment of working parents, such routines may be harder to provide, but they are no less important to the child.

He encourages parents to use quiet bedtime rituals to ease the transition. (These should not involve feeding.) Bedtime stories are a proven staple, as are songs and prayers. But you can personalize the routine and periodically update it to match your child's special interests, such as helping her put her favorite stuffed animal or doll to bed.

When the child cries, he recommends that the parent check on the child every five to ten minutes (whatever time frame is tolerable for the parent), perhaps patting and reassuring the child, but making it clear that the child is expected to stay in bed. If necessary, he recommends that the parent withdraw from the room in stages, first sitting on the bed, then in a nearby chair.

If problems persist, Dr. Minde suggests that you enlist your child's help. You can put your child's growing language and imaginative powers, as well as his growing independence, to work on the case. Explain that you need your sleep, and ask your child what would help him to stay calm when he wakes and to get back to sleep on his own. Perhaps holding and talking to his favorite teddy bear or snuggling with his favorite blanket. Make sure these items are within easy reach at bedtime.

TRAINING FOR THE TOILET

At first, it probably appears to the child that it is the toilet that's being trained (hence the misnomer "toilet training"). After all, she is typically reasonably satisfied to fill her diaper and continue on about her business. It is parents who are so enthusiastic for her to move on to the pot in support of public health.

This transition need not be Armageddon if parents remember that a body is more ready for the mind to influence its conduct when development has prepared both. Consequently, toilet training takes less time and energy when your toddler is as ready as you are. Starting too early pretty much guarantees the process will be long and messy. Many children who begin training before 18 months are not completely trained by age four, while those started around two usually are completely trained by age three.

Also, the fewer the cooks, the cleaner the kitchen. Try to minimize the number of adults the child must please. And don't be intimidated by entrance requirements for childcare programs. Training works best when it's worked out between you and your child — not an admissions officer.

Timing: Somewhere between 18 and 36 months, the child will start to notice that her dirty diaper has become a bother. She may pull at her diaper or crotch while, or just before, she empties her bladder. She'll pick a favorite corner of a room or go under a table before she quietly moves her bowels into her diaper. These are critical signs that she is making the necessary mental connection between bodily sensations and the urine or stool that is produced from them. It is easier if this behavior follows the easing of the extreme negativism of early toddlerhood. Bowel training is typically the first goal.

What Helps: Put a potty chair in the corner of her room and let her sit on it fully clothed at first, then without a diaper, a few times a day. Tell her how big people go poop and pee and let her watch a grownup using the toilet. (Stick to same sex demonstrators. Otherwise, you will create needless confusion at this age.) Tell her the potty is where she will put her poop when she is ready. Then, she can wear "big girl" pants and leave her diapers for babies. Let her play with her potty using dolls, water, whatever — the less mystery the better.

How to Proceed: Between one of these signaling behaviors and the event itself, ask — in a gently curious way — if she wants to take off her diaper and sit on the potty. If the answer is no, forget it. You will have many more chances. If she says yes, stay with her while she sits, and praise her if she "produces" (not too lavishly, however. Remember, this is her body to master, not yours.) If your child doesn't seem to be "getting it," don't force her to sit on the potty. Instead stay mildly interested and uncritical. If you change her diaper a few times and find solid stool, drop it into the potty with her help to remind her of the real deal. Try not to be too offended if she wants to touch her stool. It is obviously of great value to be the object of all this fuss, right?

Expect accidents, and that they will upset your child. If you're even more upset, you're probably pushing too hard. Sustain your child's self-regard by reassuring that: "We all have accidents while we learn to use the potty. Let's go get some dry pants." Also, expect a longer, slower process for staying dry. Girls usually don't learn day-dryness until after three, and boys learn even later.

CHAPTER 5

The Thinker

Learning, memory, curiosity, intelligence:
What they are and how they are measured.

After all this thinking about "doing," it's time to turn to how children start to master the ideas and images of their world. During this 18-month period, kids discover that causes have effects, that things can exist even if you don't see them, that you can find things if you can remember where they are, and that if you push button A on your mommy or daddy or dog or sister, you usually will get response B. Curiosity may have killed the cat, but it's still a peachy way to find things out.

Any parent who has ever been involved with a child during such learning experiments and experiences would probably admit it was easier to read the child's emotional state at any particular moment than to actually know what she was thinking or learning. The happiness or frustration, the anger or joy, the "pride smile" of accomplishment is there to see on the child's face and observe in her behavior. And you just know there's learning happening here. At such moments, how can one doubt that emotions and learning are interconnected?

And yet there is no area of child development as misunderstood by parents as the vital relationship between emotional and cognitive/intellectual development. Although this was described earlier, it bears repeating here: there are actual neural connections between the learning and feeling centers of the brain. Feeling, thinking, learning, and remembering are so tightly woven together that they are, for all practical purposes, inseparable.

And Now We Can Prove It

These connections are what the brave new world of scientific research has shown us. We can now explain in scientific terms why calm and confident children *feel* smarter, even when they aren't judged to be so by traditional measures, or why anxious and lonely children *feel* less competent, even when they aren't judged so by traditional measures. And we know why any learning transaction can be made more or less efficient by how attuned the learners and teachers are to each other emotionally. In fact, the emotional connection may matter as much as the learning itself.

Caregivers who help their children to enjoy and explore while feeling safe and loved, taking into account each child's particular temperament and appetites, are doing them a great favor in terms of predisposing them to succeed socially, creatively, and intellectually. If it feels good to the child and caregiver, and it is interesting and captivating in content and process, then it will *feel good to learn* because it simultaneously helps the child *learn to feel good*.

In this chapter we explore what we know about the thinking-feeling connection and its fellow travelers: learning, memory, intelligence, and curiosity. Then we will look at how all these attributes work together to help the young child to become a thinker, not simply a doer or a be-er.

This chapter takes us from the teachings of our latest and best research through how it plays in the real world to some ideas about how to make what we have learned work better for our 18- to-36-month-olds. Early learning drills, flash cards, hiring a bilingual nanny? I don't think so.

Through all this, I ask you to remember that there is an enormous range of "normal" in the way that very young children evolve as thinkers.

Experience-Expected

As we have seen, the parts of the brain having to do with feeling are wired to the thinking parts of the brain prior to birth. The connections don't become well organized, however, until children are born and begin to interact with their environment. That's when the brain's "information system" becomes much more sophisticated and the interconnecting brain circuitry more elaborate.

Scientists in the field of neurodevelopment use the term "experience-expected" to refer to this way that the human brain is set up — or prewired — to use life experience to maximize its growth and development. The preservation of actual neurons and the connections between them depends on the richness of a child's experience of the world, particularly at certain periods of early life.

The 18- to 36-month-old brain is intriguing not only because of the astounding proliferation of neural connections that are made during this period, but also because this happens along with, and probably because of, a very important period of specialized growth and differentiation in the brain that occurs at the same time. This growth and differentiation relate to emotional development.

We now know that, during the toddler period, the central nervous system undergoes specialized and accelerated growth in the part of the brain known as the limbic system, the part most closely connected to feeling and mood. It also develops many extra duplications of connections to the parasympathetic system, the part of the nervous system that controls everything from salivary and stomach secretion to digestion through managing smooth muscle tone in the intestines and diaphragm.

All of these systems operate outside of our conscious control, even though these are the parts of our bodies that do so much of our "feeling" for us. Learning and feeling become yoked together in an incredibly powerful way that was previously not possible because the wiring simply didn't exist at birth.

All this means that toddlers, unlike infants, now have the biological hardware to enhance their understanding of the world just as they are ready to strike off down the road on their own — a few feet at a time — for the first time.

So, just as little ones begin to need more understanding to be more on their own — and to be more aware of what they and others feel in relation to one another — the brain leaps forward to grow and give them more capacities by developing even more connections between the brain cells that already exist in the learning-feeling domain. A brilliant design.

The Emergence of Emotions

We now have the remarkable ability to actually watch the brain as it thinks and feels its way through problems, thanks to the new technologies of functional magnetic resonance imaging and positron-emission scanning. These images tempt us to think of emotion developing like some discrete, easily measurable, if not photographable, event that develops along with other linear events — something that is suddenly here where nothing used to be.

Nevertheless, as parents we must remain rooted to common sense about the emotional lives of our children. *No emotion suddenly appears from nowhere,* anymore than a skill suddenly appears from nowhere.

Still, there are developmental and growth sequences that build upon each other in fairly predictable ways. The order in which they appear is more reliable than the timetable of their appearance, but there is an orderly sequence to emotional and cognitive competencies and definable and separate feelings.

Of course, we are well aware of the order of development when it comes to motor skills. For example, we would never expect a child to start using a spoon without having first learned to smear bananas on his highchair tray, then pick up a piece of cracker between thumb and raking fingers, or pinch a pea between forefinger and thumb. Only later does "the spoon thing" get going somewhere near his mouth.

We understand all the things that make this order of skills appear in this manner — the motor and muscle sequences, the importance of concentration and success, eye-hand coordination, not to mention hunger — all are facilitators and motivators in the development and mastery of this task. We easily appreciate that handling a spoon doesn't come just from nowhere. The same is true of emotions.

Research by Robert Emde, of the University of Colorado, and others has taught us about the order in which emotions emerge — that order is more robust as a research finding than the developmental eras during which they appear. Still, it will help parents to understand where their kids are at the beginning of this era and where they will be at the end, though the rate of growth or ease of transition from one to the next is absolutely unpredictable.

By 18 months the major developmental issue is, of course, the emergence of the sense of self. Your child will feel anger and frustration primarily in the form of rage and defiance. She will feel wariness in the form of anxiety and fear, but some shame will begin to appear. Pleasure and joy are felt in the use and appreciation of affection and the pride in a positive self-image.

By 36 months the main developmental direction is the mastery of the environment through the use of fantasy, make-believe, dress-up, and play. Emotionally, children express anger and frustration through intentional hurting and retaliating. They feel and manage wariness and fear through the beginnings of guilt (the next stage after evolution of shame). Joy and pleasure now are expressed through love and pride of self, with some beginning expression of the same emotions toward others.

It's All Interconnected

Clearly, emotions, the senses, thinking, learning, and memory are woven together in a child's development. In summarizing the interconnectedness among the senses, learning, and feeling, Alan Sroufe of the University of Minnesota stresses that researchers who study emotions invariably view them as complex transactions.

Recent neurobiological research emphasizes that events which lead to emotions mixed with learning tend to occur in a particular order. It is very important that this order of events includes some way to *understand* the meaning of the events. In theory, the sequence looks like this:

Interactive stimulus > cognitive process > experienced feeling > behavior

Here's how it plays in the real world:

- ★ Something happens around the child (an unfamiliar dog lopes into, or near, the toddler's space)...

- ★ which leads to cognitive process (the child's mind recognizes it as a dog, his memory is evoked of dog-ness, including his previous experience with dogs in general, maybe even whether this is a familiar dog)...

★ which leads to experienced feeling (pleasure at seeing dog-pleasantly-remembered, or fear at being scared or threatened by dog-frighteningly-remembered)...

★ which leads to behavior (a smile rooted in pleasure, or a wail rooted in fear).

The bottom line is that the child's emotional response to any event is invariably linked to what he will learn in this interaction. The meaning of the event to the child can invite further learning and exploration if pleasurable, and withdrawal and cognitive shut-down if unpleasurable. What makes this sequence tricky is that its shape is helical, not linear. An event occurs in a context, which leads to thinking about it, which leads to experiencing emotions, which leads to behavior, which leads to further events in the context (touch the doggie or scream bloody murder), and up or down the spiral we go.

This is vitally important to understand because it means that the sensory and emotional aspects of a youngster's world and the cognitive parts of that world are seamlessly joined.

Some Ways Emotions Influence Learning

If we stop and think about it, most of us are aware that emotions — pleasant or unpleasant — impact our learning. What is curious is how often we ignore this fact in educating our children.

Developmental psychologist Michael Hoffman researched three different ways that emotion influences cognition:

1. *Emotion may cause, change or interrupt the way a child processes information.* In our dog example above, the child's mood or emotional state *before* the dog lopes in may predispose her to be open to being interested if she's feeling secure and comfortable (predisposing her further to explore dog-ness), or resistant and reluctant if she's feeling tired or irritable (predisposing her to shut down and withdraw from dog learning for today).

2. *Emotion may organize mental recall.* Pleasure in the dog encounter stimulates the recall of previous pleasurable encounters, which encourages the young explorer to reach out and touch or smell the dog, or "talk" to it, instead of simply passively looking.

3. *The emotional "charge" we attach to categories, events, and things is the product of how we felt about them in our past experiences with them.* We bring that charge to each new experience, which, in turn, may modify the charge further. The resonance between past and present pleasurable or fearful experiences with this particular dog is compared to all previous dog encounters, and emotion and learning about dog-ness accumulates in the memory-limbic-parasympathetic system where it is filed and cross-filed for the next dog encounter.

For the young child in particular, experiences are more easily understood and filed away if they are connected to the emotions contained in that event, pleasurable or not. Thunderstorms are terrifying if you are alone, wet, or hungry. Thunderstorms are neat if you are snuggled on your dad's chest, and he tells you what is happening and how safe you both are, and that the noise, lightning, and water will not "get you." Either way, boy, will you remember thunderstorms! The same is true for remembering dogs, grandmothers, songs, pictures, books, butterflies, and so forth.

The thinker can take that experience, file it, and call it up to work on later. He may construct figures in his sand pile, get water, and pour it on the carefully constructed little tableau as he roars his own thunderclap (most observers would wonder what is going *on* here?). He is working on internal images of his experience. He is talking and playing out an experience which he is thinking and feeling through. If you interrupt him, he may feel frustrated in the same way you are when interrupted in the middle of an important phone call with some irritating intrusion. "Can't you see that I…?" Most little kids resent such intrusions as they work hard to sort this stuff out.

We'll discuss the importance of play more fully in Chapter 7. Suffice it to say that in the type of play described above, kids practice and refine their inner worlds the way they practice and refine rolling or bouncing a ball, washing a doll, or pulling on a shirt. It takes time, a pleasant, unfrantic environment, some play things, and a little time to oneself. We do know that the more internal images children have at their disposal (of their own making — not Barney's or Disney's) the better they will manage in heavy weather later in life.

The seductions of the newest video, reading readiness scheme, math game, or flash card set are so slick, we can hardly resist. We never seem able to give up our belief in that magic pill. But ultimately, we serve our own creativity best when we trust our own ideas, images, metaphors, and beliefs more fully than those that are prepackaged for us — whether by a movie studio, theme park, or a toymaker.

No matter how slick, archetypal, or clever they may be, the prepackaged material eventually wears out because it's not rooted deeply enough to our own experience, culture, temperament, strengths, or weak spots. It's like the difference between the nutritional value of fruit in its own skin versus your average 10% fruit drink. Our own internal images are melded to our own experience, memory, feeling, and knowledge — marinated over a lifetime in our culture, ethnicity, lore, value, and belief systems — and that's why they *don't* wear out.

The way children accumulate those images over time is what makes this period of life so interesting. Recent memory research has built upon the pioneering work of Jean Piaget, the famous Swiss psychologist who established the idea that children learn best from comfortable, repeated, and predictable sequences. They feel pleasure at being able to predict and cause the outcomes of their actions.

This is why children delight in repetition — why they demand the same "favorite" game or song or story over and over, ad nauseam *and* absurdum. However, once they are comfortable and satisfied with a learning experience, something unexpected happens: They start to demand the new or different.

The Need for New Experiences

Imagine a toddler sitting on the kitchen floor, legs spread apart, working her way through your carefully arranged Tupperware,® opening and closing lids, vocalizing, practicing motor skills, looking for just the right fit, making things appear and disappear. How many times can she *do* this without getting bored? That depends hugely on the individual temperament of the child. Is she tolerant and mellow? She may do it for hours. Is she excitable and action oriented? Then 10 minutes might be sufficient. Still, it is fun for awhile and then, curiously, it stops being fun for no apparent reason.

But of course, there *is* a reason. There comes a point in such a sequence where the tension between mastering the old and hungering for the new builds to the point where the child's attention is broken, and learning is disrupted.

Now, imagine the same child at her grandpa's house with another set of Tupperware.® It's as though she's never seen this stuff before! Her attention is riveted, her diligence renewed. Why? Because the setting is just fresh enough, the objects, though familiar, are just different enough to regain her interest. You are watching a critical intersection between emotion and thinking — *the appetite for the novel.*

Even though children love repetition, they also are natural seekers of the new and different. Why? Because exploring and conquering the new makes children *feel good.*

Right alongside this drive to discover is the drive to control, to be an active agent for change in their world. Children want to cause events as well as learn from them. "Me do" is the most overt manifestation. The ability to cause an outcome is another big emotional win for a child. (It is for us grownups, too.) As such, cause-effect reactions are great learning experiences because the emotions attached to them are positive and powerful.

Novelty in discovering and causing requires the brain to sit up and take notice. If the level of excitement is *manageable,* the brain will file it away for future use under "interesting; let's do this again sometime."

But there are times when excitation levels are too great (e.g. the first Black Widow Spider roller coaster ride). At such times the brain seems to say: "This novelty is new alright, but it's not worth what the rest of the body was feeling at the time and should not be repeated again real soon — maybe later." Then the brain seems to file that activity under "worrisome event — too confusing — not ready for prime time."

The point here is that, like frustration, a little anxiety or worry are often part of learning from new experiences. Sometimes a child will choose to work through a worrisome situation. Sometimes not. But a bit of tension or anxiety is frequently part of certain types of learning.

Anxiety Is Part of Learning

Worries can be powerful partners in helping a child think about the world, as long as they don't swell to flood stage and wash away the child's coping strategies. If a child's worries are kept to a manageable size, especially with the help of a caregiver and a few tools, they can be effective catalysts to the mastery of learning and thinking.

Children need to learn to manage negative emotions, and to do that, they need to experience them from time-to-time at manageable levels. The anxiety-free child is a fantasy. Anxiety is an important warning signal for potential danger. Mastering both the anxiety and the thing or event that provoked it is a powerful learning experience.

Humor and light-hearted joking around are other powerful allies in managing anxiety, and toddlers especially delight in their growing capacity to make use of it. They experiment with practical jokes by playing on their own vulnerabilities, like drooling food, falling down, or putting clothes on backwards. The raucous laughter they exhibit and elicit through their clowning is not simply entertainment, but exploration of new strategies for controlling the world of emotion around them. They even mock their parents' rules and fears, running away and hiding to provoke manifest worry in their caretakers.

A LITTLE MORE SCIENCE

Developmental neuroscientists, such as my colleague Pasko Rakic at Yale University, have been studying the importance of early experience in the architecture of the mature adult brain. It is Dr. Rakic's thesis that moderate excitation in the early years, which stops short of overwhelming the early neurological coping apparatus, can actually foster the young brain's richness of associations and pathways, thereby promoting memory and information processing.

Biochemical and neurological explanations help to delineate the coupling of emotion and learning. Moods that remain stable but not too inhibitory or dampening, or too excitatory and disorganizing, are mostly maintained biochemically by the proper level and combination of the brain chemicals called neurotransmitters. These proteins are responsible for ferrying messages along and across the canals of the central nervous system.

Meanwhile, the impulses that course through that very system vary widely in intensity and complexity. Juices flow with emotion, as we well know, in the stomach, mouth, groin, eyes, armpits, and skin. But they also flow in the brain. Cognition, or learning, flows as encoded proteins and electrical impulses along thousands of fibers for any particular event, sometimes passing among and through a marinade of the aforementioned juices.

It's a complex process. Over and over again, we have had to give up the simple-minded notion that the relationship between the two is linear — that 'A' leads to 'B,' leads to 'C.' Instead, we are forever trying to do credit to the forces that underlie the most efficient and economic ways to learn and remember important things and to help us feel good about learning and remembering.

Once More:
The Importance of the Caregiver

Obviously, caregivers play a tremendous part in helping little ones cope with new experiences. For example, the *way* that the caregiver and child fit together in their joint attention to novel circumstances makes a big difference in the way the child responds to surprising events. An attuned and thoughtful caregiver can make a novel experience, like approaching the water's edge, or the dog we met earlier, an interesting adventure, full of wonder and manageable excitement.

At the same time, a caregiver who is terrified of water — and cannot conceal or manage that fear — might make that dip in the ocean feel like a frightening encounter to the child. It becomes either a delightful experience at the beach or a situation threatening to careen out of control. The caregiver's accompanying emotion can augment the event in either direction.

The importance of a child's emotional security in embarking on learning and exploring the world has been discussed in earlier chapters. The child's need for a secure base balanced with a need for independence produces an ongoing dance. Some 18-to-36-month-olds merely require a "check-in glance" with Mom or Dad before going off on their own. Other kids need a smile or a nod. Still others may need caregivers to hold a hand while they investigate a new playground. And once a child is comfortable at that playground? Some children don't care if Dad is reading the newspaper on a nearby park bench. Others may need Dad's full attention while they play in the sandbox.

What I hope to clarify is that the tension raised in the child by worrisome events can also be an energy source for intellectual growth and problem solving *if* the tension stays at a manageable level and doesn't overwhelm the small child's mind and coping strategies. No single force matters more in the management of that level of tension than the emotionally attuned presence of the child's caregiver. It is the caregiver who has the ability to help manage or regulate the experience for (and with) the child who worries too much.

The Pressure to Learn

Now that you see how learning occurs at its best and most efficient, it becomes easier to understand why the push to accelerated early learning for young children mostly misses the mark.

Rather than enhancing learning in a normally developing child, many special stimulation curricula use only a tiny portion of the learning and intelligence mechanism that is at a child's disposal — like using a 500 hp engine to run a lawn mower. And it runs the risk of burning out the engine. Parents who want to enhance their child's cognitive development should be working with the entire mechanism, rather than just a part of it.

These accelerated learning programs also take up time that could otherwise be spent on *real* learning and discovery — the kind that take root and matter for the long haul. Moreover, pressure to learn can make the experience anxious or boring rather than pleasurable. If this happens, learning begins to take on all the wrong connotations in the young child's mind and feelings. Two-year-olds don't need to learn about pressure to perform. There will be plenty of opportunity for that later in life when they are prepared for it.

Better research shows there is a serious downside to some of the current frenzy about teaching younger and younger children to read. First of all, there is no credible research that supports the idea that early instruction produces better readers. Not one of these short-term programs has been shown to have lasting benefits. Second, evidence is growing that trying to teach reading to children before kindergarten has significant negative impact. What it actually seems to do is create burnout, robbing kids of the enthusiasm for the mastery of letters, words, and phonics by driving them to acquire word skills before they have developed the appetite or palate to read. By the end of kindergarten, these prematurely pushed readers have been found to be less creative in their imagination, felt more anxious when tested for word skills, and took less pleasure overall in being in school than their peers who were in less pressure-cooker educational settings.

At this juncture, the best and most lasting learning occurs spontaneously and enjoyably, especially with the participation of a sensitive and caring adult who is responsive to the child's interests and emotions.

Moms and Dads

An area of increasing interest is the separate contributions that men and women make to shaping and encouraging their children's competence in learning and thinking. Whereas the vast majority of research has focused on the mother-child learning pair, my own research as well as that of other investigators has begun to document that children who have experienced involved and nurturing fathering receive certain cognitive advantages. Norma Radin from the University of Michigan conducted a fascinating study of four-year-olds' interactions with their parents and found that boys in particular had intelligence scores that were positively related to the degree of father nurturance. Furthermore, the opposite was also true: paternal restrictiveness or absence was negatively correlated with test scores. Dad's direct encouragement of counting and reading showed up on higher test scores.

Henry Biller's work at the University of Rhode Island shows that children who have little father involvement for whatever reason from early in their development suffer lower academic achievement scores later in school. This leads us to wonder what the father brings to academic performance that seems so important.

FATHERS AND CHILDREN

Some recent research findings about the role of fathers and their approach to parenting include the following:

★ Fathers tend stylistically to encourage problem-solving skills by letting their kids struggle with frustration a little longer before stepping in to help. (Of course, there is huge personal variation here, as there is in mothers.)

★ Fathers permit a little more emotional autonomy during learning sequences with their young children, supporting and encouraging but without the same emphasis on intimacy that is more typical among mothers.

★ Fathers tend to mix play with learning a little more successfully, from the child's point of view, allowing longer work periods.

★ Fathers' more functional ('do it because it needs to be done,' rather than 'do it because it will go better between us if you do') approach to academic work builds in the child a larger range of problem-solving skills over time that probably contributes to more lasting self-esteem.

The bottom line so far is that although fathers and mothers interact with their kids at different levels of expectation and interest, those differences seem to enrich the child's intellectual and thinking competencies in the long run. Of course, it is impossible for moms and dads to act as each other's clones, and this new area of research says that it would be a waste of time anyway. Kids seem to enjoy bridging the gap between parental styles (within reason) and benefit from the bridging along the way.

Measuring Intelligence in Young Children

As we think about how children grow in this duality of emotion and learning, it is natural to consider how learning, memory, curiosity, and intelligence can be evaluated or measured. Such measurement has begun to have widespread application as toddlers and preschool children compete for spaces in the "better" programs. There remain serious questions about whether there is any useful way to evaluate such capacities in children of this age.

One of the many questions is, "Just what are we measuring?" Howard Gardner of Harvard University has been at the forefront of identifying the many types of intelligence that people can manifest in varying degrees. Most of these are readily evident in young children (right along with a child's individual temperament and personality traits). He articulates the following categories, all of which he has identified in young children:

★Interpersonal   ★Spatial

★Linguistic   ★Musical

★Logical-mathematical   ★Intrapersonal

★Bodily-kinesthetic   ★Naturalist

Dr. Gardner has also proposed two other types of intelligence — spiritual and existential — which he is now researching. The point is that this variety clearly goes way beyond the basic skills that are tested in toddlers.

As director of assessment at a child development clinic for 20 years, I saw hundreds of children a year under the age of four who were being evaluated for problems in development, behavior, and learning. What I learned as a developmental examiner and supervisor was that the numbers and scores of developmental competence are highly suspect for any single child on any given day because they can vary significantly, depending on the child's mood or health, or the behavior of the adult accompanying the child. The child himself is the single best measure of his own competence. In other words, children should be tested over time with the same measure to actually assess their potential competence. A single evaluation is as useful as a two-legged stool.

Still, so-called "intelligence testing" is used by some programs to "screen" applicants for more competitive childcare or preschool programs. However, there is no place for the use of intelligence screening in this age group because the rate of development is so fast and uneven that the number scores, if you could even get any reliable ones, could change the next month in either direction.

Consequently, responsible preschool programs interview children individually or in small groups, talk to their parents at length, and look for individual skill areas that would help the child feel successful in that particular setting. Problem solving, social skills, and communication abilities are generally evaluated pretty subjectively by experienced early childhood professionals. Only then can the fit between child and program be thoughtfully evaluated and an appropriate decision made.

So What Should You Do?

Now that you have all this information about intelligence and learning, what should you do with it?

In general, the simpler the better. Rocket science is for rockets. Here are some suggestions about how to enrich your child's predisposition to explore her feelings about her world through play and curiosity. For the sake of brevity, I call this *learnplay*. But first let's return to the toddler and the dog and review once again the importance of the caregiver.

At each moment in the various scenarios we described, the outcome of the learning-feeling duet could have been significantly altered by the behavior of the caregiver. In the situation of the frightened toddler, imagine the parent moving in close, arm around frightened child, comforting and soothing. If the caregiver thinks the dog and child might have a chance of rapprochement, the adult might settle the child, then see if he is still interested. If so, the adult might call the dog over for a pat, introducing the dog in a less frightening, more welcoming way.

Or imagine the reverse: The child is fine and interested and it is the parent who is afraid of the approaching animal. The parent tenses and recoils physically, verbally, or both, and the child's interest and curiosity are shaken. He may stop in his tracks, just slow down, or turn to bury his face in his parent's legs, depending on his nature and the degree of his distress. In any case, this shared experience has a different outcome: The caregiver's feeling state had cognitive implications for the child's experience.

LEARNPLAY

★**For Physical Play.** Assuming the 18-month-old is a steady walker, give her access to climbing toys both inside and out, swings, and push-pull toys. Stairs are perfect and irresistible, but only with supervision. Wading pools (supervised 100% of the time) are sensory-stimulation dreams. Pushing toys and doll carriages are great for strength and balance, while pulling plastic or wooden wheeled animals can also delight.

Large trucks or vehicles for scooting around on or in are great for body confidence. However, I concur in the recommendation of the American Academy of Pediatrics against walkers. These toys cause 25,000 injuries annually — way too dangerous. No electrical conveyances, either. These are also dangerous, teach nothing, and are absurdly expensive. Buy books instead.

★**For Small Muscle Development.** A sturdy chair at the sink or a pan of water evokes extended exploration with sinking, floating, melting, and dissolving. Ice cubes, watercolors, soap for bubbles. Finger-painting mats combine the interest in the texture and feel of paints with the visual delight of their colors. Play dough satisfies the drive to manipulate, tear, pound, feel, and dominate. Sturdy paper for scribbling (both sides) should be plentiful, and big, chunky crayons (washable and non-toxic) for small hands.

★**For Combined Motor and Problem Solving Activities.** Dress children for dirt and take them outside for some valuable messing around. Getting dirty is a treat for toddlers, and mud, clay, and sand are irresistible. Let them gather sticks, stones, shells, make piles, and investigate. For the kids who are texture-sensitive and like to stay on the clean side, give them a sandbox of washed sand.

Cleaned up and back inside, satisfy their desire to manipulate by providing blocks of varying sizes and shapes for building and knocking down over and over and over… Nesting toys and dolls can be particularly interesting to them right now. Given how hard they are working on separation and autonomy issues, being the boss of making things appear and disappear can be great fun! Blocks, toys, and pieces that fit, thread, or hook together are especially rewarding.

★**For Language and Communication.** Large, cardboard picture books with colorful, detailed illustrations that you can look at together (and occasionally chew on) fit this era wonderfully. Turn the pages slowly and draw your child's attention to each figure by pointing and sounding interested yourself in what is being depicted. Simple descriptions of the figure or the action will keep her interested. Leave these in accessible places in your home or apartment if possible so kids can pull them out themselves. A few left in the crib also are a good idea.

Human figure dolls and stuffed animals are great ways for kids this age to explore how their world fits. Mommies and daddies are put into trucks and driven to "go work"; stuffed animals can be adored or reviled, depending on the need to work out a feeling; a baby doll can be fed or smashed, depending on how a child might be feeling about a sibling, all without legal consequences.

★**Finally, for Unscheduled Time.** The capacity to be alone is an essential skill for all of us to develop. The ability to be alone without being lonely gives us time to rest, reflect, and relax without necessarily needing to sleep. This is an era when children can begin to develop this skill. Exhaustion, both physical and emotional, creates overwhelming tensions, and quiet time is one of the best antidotes.

Your own ideas about how to use what you now know about the importance of integrating emotion and learning in everyday moments with your child are probably better than anything I could advise for you personally. But here are some ideas and suggestions that might help you customize those ideas.

★ *Talk with your child.* Hopefully, you have been doing that since the moment she was born. Chat with her about what you and she are doing. She'll become part of the conversation sooner if you express to her what you love about being a parent.

★ *Encourage curiosity* and understand that repetition is a good thing for him, boring though it might be for you. The neurological basis for the insistence on the familiar lies in the fact that when synaptic connections are repeatedly activated by the same stimulation, they become immune from elimination during the brain's pruning process. They survive to become permanent neural connections that enhance learning. So go ahead and do what your child likes — over and over. This is a good rut to be in.

★ *Simply being nearby* and available while your child plays on his own is so important, as is your willingness to interact. So get down on the floor and stay awhile. Of course, this is hard for working parents, but the effort is worth it.

★ *Nothing beats reading.* Children don't learn interactive, conversational language from TV because it does not respond to *them.* Language and eventually reading are learned from being actively engaged in speaking and reading with others — hearing parents and caregivers talk to each other and waiting for the child to respond.

★ *Children learn best* in the context of their daily lives and when the amount and kind of stimulation fits their temperament, level of development, interests or preferences, and mood. Pressure to perform or conform to high expectations can lead to stress that can sabotage learning through burnout and confusion. Edward Ziegler, the pre-eminent Yale psychologist and founder of Head Start, has emphasized repeatedly how very, very hard it is to raise anybody's IQ.

★ *Young children* do not need to be taught how to think. Science is careening ahead pursuing fascinating findings and ideas about how, even whether, children this age actually do think. But our ignorance dominates our knowledge embarrassingly. We are still understanding why they even *want* to think in the first place. Is it like walking or talking, unfolding in due course when the maturational timekeeper tells the mind-body duality, "Johnny: it's time?"

★ *The five-second check-in.* Since most of us don't spend our days staring end-lessly at our toddlers and preschoolers, it is important that you take a few seconds to assess the mood, or state your child is in *before* you join in his doings, ask him to do something, or simply interrupt him. This is the feel-ing state that will determine his ability to understand or comply with what-ever you might need, no matter how small. If you are not tuned in, he probably won't hear (i.e. learn).

★ *Join your child.* Follow her lead in activities she is already involved in. Don't take over — it will turn her off. But if you want her to learn, become a part-ner in the exploration she has begun. Add a ball to hide in the pots and pans scene, or move close and take her hand if she is wary of a dog on a walk. Don't instantly rescue (unless safety is an immediate concern) because you will lose one of those interesting moments of tension that could be mastered, leading a child to a wider, more complex understanding of the world.

★ *If your child balks* at a "learning" moment with you, it could mean you didn't read the five-second check-in right. Back up and let your child know you know what she is feeling first. ("I guess you weren't quite through," or "It's hard to have to stop when you are having fun doing X.") When the feeling domain feels appreciated, then the learning domain is less burdened.

★ *If your child needs* redirection after you have connected with his mood or feeling, ask softly what he might enjoy doing. If you still have no luck, make two suggestions of things he might do and help him choose. He will proba-bly need some pump-priming from you, since you can manage your own mood apart from his. Remember, *how* you are in such moments, is as impor-tant as *what* you do.

★ *If it's important* for you to initiate an activity that will bring you pleasure and you know it could be good for your child, like reading or going for a walk, stabilize your own mood first. Only then can you help your child reg-ulate hers. Once done, then she can crawl up on your lap or get out the door and learn. For some kids, it's the other way around. But for the majority, in the feeling and learning dance, it isn't always possible to say who is leading.

CHAPTER 6

Communication Through Show and Tell

Language explosions. Behavior that speaks when words fail.
Saying what they mean and understanding when they can't.

My 23-month-old niece, Jenzi, was a chatty, confident toddler with a mop of blonde hair and a sturdy frame. She loved company, bidding for complete and undivided attention whenever any of us were in sight of her engaging smile. Jenzi was warm, persistent, and verbal enough that she generally got her way with most adults, engaging them with entertaining discourse, regardless of whether or not it made sense. Her constant companion in her daily journeys was a deeply beloved, if ill-repaired, little chenille doll whom she named "Jenzistoomuch." It was a charming, but totally mystifying name.

As a new student of personality development in young children at the time, I was intrigued by the naming of her doll. Then a predictable sequence made itself known. After Jenzi provoked pleasure or laughter in a grandparent or uncle with some cute little misspeak, such as calling the toilet bowl a "fwushuh," the common phrase of affection was, "Oh, Jenzi, you're too much!" Aha! What is happening here? Why would she give this descriptive phrase, provided by family members for her pleasing behavior, to her doll — an object imbued with the magic to comfort and soothe when upset, to reassure when frightened, and to sleep with when giving up the day? Language is such a wonderful mystery!

The acquisition of language is what separates infancy from toddlerhood. In fact the Latin root of our word "infancy" means "not yet speaking." To some parents the advent of speech is a huge relief. *Now* I know what you need, or don't need, or are upset about. Their toddlers may feel the same — *now* I can tell you what I *really* like on my cereal. To other parents it is less jubilant because infancy is undeniably over. No more wordless intimacies or private chats where I talk for us both. How time does fly. In certain Asian cultures, the nonspeaking child is considered more wise and vigilant than the speaking child, and the advent of speech is met with sighs as the cause for some sadness.

In this chapter, we will explore how children develop the ability to say what they need with words and behavior, sometimes apart and sometimes together. Then we'll look at what happens during these 18 months to the connection between language development and emotions as children get better control of their impulses and feelings

Talking and Feeling

Before bringing you up to speed on the freshest research on the neurophysiology of speech and language and the fascinating connection between emotional differentiation and language development, we need to think together about what talking has to do with feeling, and vice versa.

Words do more than communicate thoughts and facts. They allow us to organize and categorize those thoughts and facts — just as numbering systems allow us to do arithmetic after we've run out of fingers and toes to count on, or file names let us access previous work on a particular topic.

Children weeks old begin to bubble and coo, then move to squeals and squeaks, then repetitive tongue and lip movements, all in a fairly predictable sequence. As children age, they spend a fair amount of time experimenting and playing with sounds.

They play with giggles, cooing, wailing, grunting, moaning, bubble blowing on their way to their first word, just as they play with their feet or body parts on their way to sitting up, crawling, and walking. The pleasure gained in the mastery of sounds helps drive development forward. Be honest. You know those sounds are fun to make because you mimic them just to see that little face light up.

While infants begin uttering sounds for the sheer delight of doing so, they won't attach meaning to those sounds until around 12 months. Once this happens, children discover the power of words to cause action — saying "Mama" is likely to bring Mom to the scene. Children also discover that words can call forth mental images of the people or things the words mean — saying or thinking "Mama" will bring up a mental picture of Mom. Such images can be very comforting to a child when Mom isn't physically present, such as at bedtime. Most parents are familiar with children's nighttime chants, a mix of words and syllables that call up images of the child's world that are temporarily out of sight once the lights go out. While the uttered name may not magically or instantly produce Mom, the mental image or picture attached to the name provides important comfort until she actually appears.

The Language Explosion

Development rates vary, of course, but generally a language explosion occurs around 18 months. At that time, most children start adding new words at an incredible rate, giving them a vocabulary of 1,000 to 2,000 words by the time they are two. At 18 months they also are likely to combine words into short phrases — "want juice," "no sleep," "go bye-bye."

Grammar, too, is rapidly acquired. Our brains seem to be naturally prone to, and capable of, the grammar and the organization that makes language work. By 24 and 30 months, children have a basic sense of their language's internal structure or grammar, usually placing pronouns, nouns, and verbs in the right order.

As vocabulary expands to include verbs and adjectives as well as nouns, language moves from naming objects into describing what they do and how they do it. This, in turn, sets the stage for using words *in place of* the objects they name. This is a very important development because it is *the cornerstone of judgment, reasoning, managing impulses, and inhibiting action.* Armed with the right words, a child who doesn't like big dogs needs only to be told that there is a "big dog" in the backyard at a neighbor's house to understand what awaits him should he venture out the back door.

All this makes it clear that the more a child wants to convey about his experience, the sooner his speech will develop. The urgency of first words is directly related to the tension created in the child over *being understood*. It literally *feels good* in one's mind and body to be understood, not simply in one's ears.

Even as adults we will talk "until blue in the face," referring to our failure to stop and breathe until we *are* understood. When at last we are understood, we relax physiologically. The toddler feels the same swings of passion under these circumstances.

Making Life Easier

Once children start to use even a little language, everyone benefits. Child reading and child rearing become much easier. There is more accurate and pleasurable communication between child and parent. More important is the feeling of mastery and control the toddler begins to have over her own impulsive life.

The child who learns to yell "doggie!" whenever he sees his unpredictable neighborhood pet, can connect his own internal mixture of excitement about petting an affectionate animal with the worry and impulse to run away if it barks too suddenly. Using the spoken word that stands for the whole experience of dog-ness, including the pleasurable and the worrisome, he has some control over what will happen next. He neither has to run away or run toward the dog to see what his fur feels like. He begins to understand and remember from time to time the power over the world's events that words have.

Imagine how frustrating that same scene is for the child without language. As a clinician I have seen hundreds of young children brought by parents who were concerned about their child's failure to talk. Yet even in the absence of useful speech, the drive by most of these children to communicate is so strong that they have developed a large repertoire of gestures, gesticulations, pushings and pullings, grunts and groans to communicate their needs, pleasures, and fears. But their frustration at their limited language is usually palpable.

In the great majority, speech evolves in time. The relief is wonderful all around, but is most deeply felt in the child. Still, the presence of these gestural "languages" reminds us that speech is but one form of communication, and that children don't instantly abandon one when they develop the other.

The "Bye-Bye" Girl

At 21 months, Genny will start saying "bye-bye" with an upturned query in her tone as she sees her parents preparing to leave for work. Before this skill, her face wrinkled up into a scowl just before tears melted her eyes, and a piercing wail ended the sequence. Now, with her words, she takes their leavings more peacefully. Her questioning statement begs an answer and she usually gets one. Before speech, it was mostly guesswork about what she was thinking or feeling. It's as though *she* has become the boss of separations and departures, not her parents.

Another place a child's language is a huge help to parents is in helping children check some of their own impulses.

Learning to Play It Safe

George loves to watch the wood-burning stove glow with warmth and listen to the crackling bark. The first time he said the word "hotuh!" was the morning after his father had stopped him dead in his tracks on the way to touch the stove with an emphatic, "Don't touch, George – *hot!*"

For three weeks after he had said his first "hotuh," he played this game: In the mornings when the stove was cool, he would reach out his hand and walk toward the stove, sometimes looking to see who was watching. He would then say "hotuh!" and stop about two feet from the stove. If an adult joined in his game, he enjoyed it, but their partnership was not essential. He was controlling the frightening burning stove and his impulse to explore it through this highly effective game. It *felt* important to him to figure it out, he *learned* how to do it, and he *said* the right word in the right way at the right time for it all to come together.

George is using words — both their meaning and the act of speaking them — as a tool to control his behavior. He uses his words and his repeated approaches to the stove to drill home his father's message that he must not touch. And he succeeds in stopping himself. This is how words are central to judgment and inhibiting behavior.

In the following sequence, Stanford University psychologist Ellen Markman has shown how emotions work. She describes a chain of events that helps us understand the place of language in the stream of behavior.

- ★ **The chain starts with an action (a stove burning), which leads to…**
- ★ **A tension to react or do something (the impulse to touch), which leads to…**
- ★ **A need to explain or understand the tension or discover its meaning (it's not enough to just watch), which leads to…**
- ★ **Assigning a feeling to the particular tension (pleasure in discovery that is too dangerous to allow), which leads to…**
- ★ **The use of language to describe the end point of the process ("hotuh," learned from the countless hearings preceding his first use of the word!).**

Such rich processes are how children increasingly use language to make sense of their world and their experiences. These processes also are what neurophysiologists credit with the post-birth development and increasing complexity of brain structures. Just think of all the social, cognitive, emotional, and cultural factors that went into George's first "hotuh!" If you tried to diagram all the parts of the brain that had to be up and running and connected to each other for that to happen, the circuitry pathways would be very dense. Never again is so large a portion of the brain's and mind's resources devoted to the accumulation of language. So, make hay while the sun shines.

There is a wide range of speech and language development that is considered normal. Early or later speech within that range is not linked to intelligence or reading ability. However, you should expect to see the following in your child:

★**18 months:** Use of single words and phrases such as "bye-bye;" use of nouns, verbs, and gestures, alone or in combination, to convey meaning; ability to follow simple instructions.

★**24 months:** Use of two- and three-word phrases; increased understanding of what others are saying.

★**30 months:** Use of plural nouns and sentences that contain negatives; asks what and where questions; names and understands a color or two.

★**36 months:** Knows a familiar tune or song; asks why and who questions; understands 'under,' 'behind,' and 'on'; can designate the actions associated with objects in pictures.

Speech can be delayed for a number of reasons. However, it is essential to check out possible medical reasons, including impairments to a child's hearing, ability to coordinate the muscles in the tongue, lips, and mouth, or to process language properly. Some auditory problems can be greatly relieved if treated early enough. Once medical problems have been ruled out, other reasons for delayed speech include:

★**Preference for gestural language.** Over-attentive parenting can make it less necessary for a child to speak since the parent is talking for everyone. Refusal to speak can also be a form of negativism. So stand back a bit to encourage the little guy to work with words to let you know what he means and wants.

★**Bilingual households.** Children raised with more than one language can often take up to an extra year to start speaking as they grapple with the sounds and vocabulary of two tongues. But they will typically speak both languages fluently when they finally do start talking — a nice reward for the wait!

As to speech impairments, it's important to distinguish trial-and-error mistakes from real problems. It is perfectly normal for children to stutter or stammer, or to get syllables or sounds reversed as they are mastering language. However, you should consider a professional evaluation if these problems persist or if you see difficulties in any of the following areas:

★**Sound quality** (such as a high pitch, excessive nasal quality, or shrill sound)

★**Conversation** (an inability to follow and respond to another or to take turns in communicating)

★**Meaning** (excessive repetition of words with no context or no communicative purpose or intent)

★**Responsiveness** (regularly under- or over-reacting when spoken to)

Speech therapy is increasingly used. Being on the safe side is generally a good idea. But in today's push to accelerated learning, I have some concern that children who are otherwise developing just fine are being plucked from the playroom and put in a therapist's office with questionable net gain.

Facets of Language Explosion

While language grows exponentially during this period, sometimes it still doesn't seem to keep pace with all the other facets of growth that are occurring. Part of the problem is that children this age understand much more language than they speak, and frustration can reign when they can't find the right words for something important. In these instances, a parent's ability to put the child's fear or frustration or hurt into words is magic in its ability to soothe, heal, and solve problems.

A Cat in the Lap

Matthew at 19 months was fascinated by the kitten in his cousin's lap. His eyes were wide open, and he was so still you couldn't see him breathing. He wouldn't reach out and touch or say anything, despite his mother's attempt to help him engage. After 20 minutes, it was time to go, his cousin got out of the chair to leave, and Matthew dissolved in tears. What the heck was the matter?

Finally, his dad guessed it — Matthew *did* want to touch the cat after all. When Dad asked, he said "dutch" (touch?). He did and smiled warmly. A helpful word had turned chaotic uncertainty for the adults into orderly behavior for Matthew.

A big growth in language occurs when children are able to communicate both physical and emotional pain to a parent. This takes the relationship up a big notch as language provides an outlet and an avenue for help, worry, fear, excitement, and loneliness.

As this sophistication grows, words become not just labels, but a kind of shorthand to categorize and sort memories and meaning. As the categories grow, they offer an ever-richer variety of alternatives.

As the options open up, they give children more avenues to initiate action. Being active in getting one's needs met is a huge and critical boost to one's self-esteem. Language and the feeling connected to it provide an exponential surge to the toddler's ability to feel mastery over his world. Just as being cared for and loved as an infant helps one feel valued and worthy, being talked to as an infant and toddler makes one feel worthy of conversation and dialogue. "You are worth talking to" quickly becomes "you are worth listening to." What accumulates over time is that the child begins to "expect well" of those who talk and listen to him, enhancing the neuro-biological readiness to talk and be heard.

The Emotions of Language Development

This leads very naturally to the heart of the chapter: the relationship between emotion and language development. The pioneer in the field, Robert Emde, at the University of Colorado, studied this connection for decades, beginning with how young, newly speaking children come to acquire the ability to label emotions and distinguish them from one another. He paved the way for the understandings we now have about how thinking, social transactions, relationships, and emotion converge powerfully in the second year. It is here, in the realm *between* people, that children feel the desire and passion to share what they feel and think, especially about their desires, feelings, and beliefs about life *together* with these important people.

One of the country's most distinguished researchers and thinkers about speech and language development, Lois Bloom, at Columbia University, has begun to change the way we understand the huge role that emotional development and expression play in promoting language development in the early years of life. She has determined that what drives language development is the overlap between:

1. **The *effort* to communicate** – the work of being aware of the world around, and of thinking enough about experiences to want to communicate something about them, and

2. **The feeling of *engagement*** – the social desire to communicate within a human relationship.

It works best for the child to feel that what she has to say matters both to her and to the person who hears it. It is the talking and feeling child that gets herself across, feels heard, and wants to say more the next time. Dr. Bloom's research should reassure parents who resist the urge to artificially drive vocabulary development: *Language and emotional expression are most efficiently coupled when children learn to talk about those things they have feelings about.*

Dr. Bloom noted that toddlers were more likely to talk about what they were *doing* as opposed to what they were *feeling* when they were busy playing with blocks rather than people. There were fewer pouts and frowns, verbal exasperations, or jubilance, as they built their block designs or stacked their rings, pots, or pans. This type of "neutral" play seemed to promote early language learning. Kids whose play was highly emotional and contained fewer neutral sequences seemed to learn language later.

Bottom line for parents: your toddlers need a balance of neutral, skill-building play with play that also expresses feeling and emotion (costumes, doll corner, etc.). Such a balance permits language learning to benefit from the best mix of effort and engagement.

The Symbolic Power of Words

As children's language ability grows, the symbolic power of words and the child's growing memory lead to another transformation. Just a few short months ago, your toddler was easily distracted from an upset, which she promptly forgot. Now, she won't so easily forget what she wanted because she can remember it, mostly because of the sorting and labeling power of the words she is learning.

Moreover, she will want to remember, because getting the things that are important to her matter much more to her increasingly mature self. Wanting their own way is an important avenue for children to exert their autonomy. Negativism and all those "noes" are just part of the game. While it can be bothersome for parents, it is a clear testament to their child's growth and to the central role of language in that process.

Such resistance is just one aspect of the transformation that comes by the time a child is three. At that point, many facets of development begin to gel — an explosion of coming together and maturation. As the "self" evolves, bolstered by language and newly emerging emotions, such as shame, guilt, and pride, a child begins to achieve a balance between the drive to follow every impulse and the ability to check those drives. If this balance has been encouraged and nurtured, the child is truly blessed with a strong foundation of language and learning skills reinforced and modulated by maturing emotions.

PRACTICAL STEPS FOR LANGUAGE DEVELOPMENT

★ If your child is not talkative, pay close attention. Quiet toddlers *mean* something with their quietness. Is your child engaged in work, needing to remain verbally still to focus her effort? Are they not enthusiastic enough about conversation in general? Are you? Are they temperamentally quiet? Are you doing too much talking, or not enough? Get yourself to think about it. It generally helps quiet kids to gently encourage them to converse. Humor is especially helpful for the shy ones, but never mock or shame their attempts at speech.

★ Follow your toddler's lead, and get on his bandwagon when he's on a roll. Narrate the scene and describe his own behavior back to him; "Sam loves to…," or "Sam is sad his Mommy has to leave…," or "Sam is so happy to play with his blocks." Don't overdo, but do. It shows your toddler that you understand him and appreciate his inner world, not just his blue eyes. Soon enough it will be a dialogue.

★ Funny as early speech may sound, don't exploit the humor of it at your child's expense. Whenever a new skill emerges, it is at its most raw and tender (remember your first public poetry recital?). Stuttering and stammering are normal when children are learning to speak. Treat early language with the respect it deserves. It has taken tremendous effort to get here. Say it back correctly if you figure out what it is, but don't "correct" too much. Be patient. Early language should feel good to both of you, and not because it's right, but because it is intimate communication between two people who feel deeply connected to each other. Soon she won't be saying much if her first words always are being corrected.

★ Allow quiet play. This may seem paradoxical when language is the goal, but rest and reflection that are restorative and interesting become important when so much effort is being expended in new skill.

★ Talk about your own feelings and how they got that way in a simple and straightforward manner. Children who have never heard their parents talking about how or what they are feeling on a day-to-day basis face an uphill climb to develop useful understandings about language and emotion. Say things like:

"I was sad when my friend forgot to come over…"

"I felt happy to get that nice letter from Grandma…"

"It scared me when the truck got so close."

Simple, clear, and to the point. The feeling in your voice will capture your toddler's interest, so don't be too surprised to see her staring at you at first. It gives her the words to match the emotion she reads in you and will eventually identify in herself.

★ Read, read, and read some more. To them, to yourself, to each other. Then talk about what you read. It is the organic garden where new words grow.

CHAPTER 7

Play, Learning, and the Dawn of Imagination

When play is more than fun and becomes the work of understanding.
Figuring out the real from the not-so-real.

The genius of child development specialist Selma Fraiberg was to get it right: The young child is the first magician. As the center of his own universe, he believes that the sun rises because he is ready to play with it, and it sets because he is no longer amused. Sadly, the parent's grim but essential task is to slowly start to say it ain't so. In between those perceptions is that last great imaginary time and place.

In this chapter we will explore that time and place where play, learning, and imagination are fellow travelers. We'll look at why play matters so much in the growth of every child's personality and creativity, not to mention her permanent sense of self-respect. We will investigate the importance of play in this era as the work of understanding experience, and why the real world seems so highly overrated to children, even though that's where the real people are. Not that play can't also be enjoyable, but we must understand that, for the young child, it's a lot more than entertainment.

Play and Learning

If we have missed the boat on the critical relationship between learning and emotion, we're bound to miss the next boat, too — the vital connection between play and learning. For most parents, children's play is just that and no more — diversion or entertainment. Kids do seem to like it after all, and their pleasure in devoting hours to play, make-believe, and following their imaginations is usually obvious.

But to think that play matters *only* in so far as it brings pleasure is to miss the forest for the trees. Play is ultimately about learning. True enough, learning can be great fun, but it so often isn't in our schools and worklife, that it is hard to remember that play has its roots in the delights found in the cabinet under the kitchen counter, or the hedgerow around the backyard, or Dad's desk drawer.

And *all play is educational play,* just as all television is educational television. We may not be happy about the curriculum, but the learning happens just the same. Good stuff, bad stuff, stupid stuff. It all gets played and learned.

One of the interesting findings in a recent poll conducted by Zero to Three, National Center for Infants, Toddlers and Families, is that many parents don't fully appreciate the connection between play and cognition. They certainly know that a baby's intelligence can be affected by how they, as parents, interact with their children. But according to the poll, parents of young children significantly underestimate the power that play has in enriching a child's learning competence. Furthermore, they thought their role as play partner was much less important than it was as a learning partner. *Not true.* You will see throughout this chapter just how important you are in the realm of play.

All Play Means Something

The reason that children love to play is precisely because it does *mean* something. They come to it very naturally from the beginning months of their life.

Developmentalists call the first play activities "circular reactions." That's when an infant repeatedly kicks the inside of her crib to get the attached mobile to move or tosses toys out of the playpen over and over, endlessly fascinated by whatever ruckus ensues.

Later, the child moves to "fantasy play." Here, as noted in earlier chapters, the 18- to 36-month-old may recast a personal experience in symbolic form using toys or dolls. In both forms of play, the reward comes from the action, and repetition of the actions leads to mastery. Here's that emotion-cognition link. Of course, the child is learning all the while.

In fact, a vast amount of a child's total learning comes through play, both alone and with you. What are some of the things children learn through play?

⋆ **They learn what is soft and hard, cold and warm, scratchy or smooth, as they touch and manipulate everything within reach.**

⋆ **They learn what is heavy and light, as they heft and fling things about their world.**

⋆ **They learn what is sour and sweet, as they mouth, suck, and drool their way though everyday life.**

⋆ **They learn what is quiet and loud, pleasing or raucous, as they scream and coo, or rub and smash.**

⋆ **They learn what works and doesn't work, as they pull and push, fit, stack, and destroy.**

One of the most important things they learn through all this tireless trial and error is how to connect events, feelings, memories, thoughts, and learning together into experience and to file it away in their brains under certain symbols. Miraculously, this all starts to happen well before they have command of spoken language. Simply stated, through play, they learn to symbolize their experience.

The Symbols of Play

Think about it. Their play helps them understand that things can stand for other things — that keys or shoes can stand for "Daddy," that her purse or underwear can stand for "Mommy," that a leash or collar can stand for a dog. It is quite amazing, really, because there is no way we can ever achieve that *for* our kids. They simply have to sort it out on their own.

How? As a child rummages through the bottom of the closet and pulls out a familiar pair of big, old shoes, someone who takes notice in the sequence of the child's play will say the word "Daddy," and probably more than once. The child plays (with pleasure) as she pairs them up, hefts their weight, maybe even struggles to put on those size 12s. And the "power" word she hears in this whole scenario is "Daddy." After the memory and pleasure centers in the brain connect with the word heard for this experience, the experience gets filed (pleasantly) under "daddy" or "shoes" or "smelly feet"— probably all three.

But most importantly, the experience gets remembered *(learned),* and soon the play starts to symbolize the child's experience with any or all of the parts of this scene. *Which* experience is hard to predict, be it remembering her father when he is gone, classifying pairs of things that belong together, or the raw joy of exploring. But the experience now has some kind of symbol connected to it, thanks to play.

Moreover, experience gets symbolized and images fixed through play in a way that the child can create new symbols over time. He combines and reshapes old ones, or uses them in novel ways. This capacity to manipulate and change them gives him wonderful new tools for elaborating his own experience and understanding of the world and his place in it. This remarkable capacity is what we call "imagination."

On the "Phone"

Two-year-old Olivia stands at the pretend kitchen counter, right hand on her hip, animatedly talking into the plastic banana she is holding up to her left ear.

This is really a magical scene, once you realize that the real phone is completely missing and superfluous. Olivia's mind obviously has the theory that talking on the phone is a much larger event than holding an earpiece in the hand. It's social, it's done in the kitchen, it's emotionally interesting, and it means something. All this adds up to such importance that a plastic banana can easily be pressed into service as the imagined portable phone. Yes, she might be missing her mommy right then, or calling her daddy, or making plans to visit grandma. But whatever is happening, it's hers.

The Dawn of Imagination

Few parents miss the fact that imagination is part of play, but it is discouraging how many parents fail to understand the importance of imagination to all aspects of the child's development. Perhaps this is why too many parents and educators consider art and music programs "frills" and allow these programs to be cut from a school's curriculum when money is tight. More on that later.

Imagination surfaces when the child takes what she has learned through play about how her past experiences can be symbolized, and starts to "imagine" things, beyond mere repetition. She does this by manipulating these very symbols in new, not-yet-experienced ways. This is a fabulous moment, because it is a first ray in the sunrise of creativity. If you can get things to stand for *other* things, there is no end — *no end* — to what the child, through play can figure out about her place in the world.

Since this happened in us so long ago, it's hard to remember what the elation felt like. In fact, because we were thinking in mental, rather than symbolic or even word-based images at that time, we probably don't remember it at all. (As you may recall from the chapter on language, words help us to fix mental images in our heads, which is probably why the earliest pre-verbal childhood memories are so sketchy. Without a word or file name, the file is lost.)

But this elation is precisely what children feel as they learn to think in their pre-verbal, non-, or just-barely-speaking world (the average 18-month-old has 22 words). If you need an image to freshen your memory of how compelling the desire to play/learn is, take an 18- to 20-month-old on a walk and see how much playing he is compelled to do. Be patient about how long the walk will take!

Imagination and Comfort

Playing is a need. And the child of around 20 months is still very much a willing slave to her needs. As long as the young mind is dominated by needs, such as hunger, pain, strong emotion, anger, fear of separation, and immediacy of satisfactions, including the need to play, mental activity develops in the service of these needs.

We see this, for example, in the way children often need and name "transitional companions" — those beloved dolls, stuffed animals, or blankets that they carry about for a time, such as "Jenzistoomuch" from Chapter 6. The importance of these creatures and their imagined powers should not be taken lightly. Most parents have experienced at least a few desperate moments when a child needs and calls for such an object, and it cannot be located.

The Magic "Softie"

Donny was so exhausted after his full day at a family picnic that his usual playtime with his dad after dinner was one disaster after another. Finally, in desperation, he wailed for his "DZOFDIE!" (His word for "softie," his small, crimson-red, bean-bag toy.) When it could not be located immediately — and I do mean immediately — by his parents and the combined search force of second cousins and uncles, he crossed over from despair to meltdown. But when reunited with his beloved softie, he was instantly calmed. The source of the toy's "magic" should be clear at this point. The child's *imagination* had imbued it with such special significance that it surpassed human contact.

Donny's father was worried that his son was too dependent on his "softie" and, on occasion, tried to "lose" it, thinking Donny would need it less if he had it less. Wrong. It served a critical, if short-lived, purpose for Donny as he struggled to become more independent in his world. Whatever its specific meaning, Dzofdie was imagined to stand for comfort, security, peace, and contentment — everything that Donny's father would want for him. What bothered Donny's father so much was that it seemed at times that Donny needed Dzofdie more than him! Ah, those tender male egos. True, many fathers love to tease in their play with their young ones, but I encouraged him to find another way. This talisman was a little too sacred right now to be "lost," even in play.

Selma Fraiberg humorously and accurately compares the child's parents and other adults at this time to "missionaries," bent on replacing their child's magic with reason and truth and trading pleasure for reality. She advises them not to be zealots and to heed the practice of real-life missionaries who allow new converts to keep some of their old talismans and beliefs, helping to direct them to good use.

Imagination and Fear

We've already seen how children in their second year — on their way to an independent self — begin to develop internal emotional controls. We've looked at how language helps them understand that their actions have consequences (good and bad), that sometimes they have to wait for what they want, and that the things they do can make the people they love feel wonderful or lousy.

But we've also seen that play, with or without language, is important to their emotional landscape. Through play, they not only explore positive experiences and feelings, but they learn to deal with painful ones, as well. In fact, the power of play to help a child manage anxiety and worries is considerable!

Has little Matthew been experiencing separation anxiety? He can take a mommy doll and baby doll, wrap them up or tape them together if he really wants them to stay together "always." Is Brandon worried about that new German shepherd next door? He can throw a stuffed doggy across the room if he needs to act out his fear of the dog or to "boss it around" without fear of reprisal.

As with all "magic," imagination is hard to control. Worries accompany the omnipotence of this era, and the management of anxiety becomes a major task and preoccupation. This, too, is normal and expected. The fear of the dark is a good example of how a child comes to master such anxieties.

Rarely is such a fear a direct result of something traumatic that actually happens in darkness. More commonly, the fear is rooted in the visual experience of being alone, and the aloneness engenders a sense of fear and danger. The imaginings begin to cascade, and the need to summon "help" seems overwhelming. The child who knows help will come has a different experience than the child who knows no one is likely to come. Again, experience and genetics conspire to render each child unique in this circumstance.

Even Halloween becomes a problem where it wasn't before. Previously, it was just an unending, if bewildering, source of sweets. But now, thanks to new levels in understanding, it can be truly menacing. Beloved Uncle Tommy becomes a serial killer under the wrong mask, and it takes a lot of reassurance before the child wants to sit on his lap again.

The explanation for this change? The very complexity of the new symbols of experience that fuel such wonderful imagination, play, and learning turn against the child because now he *believes* bad things can happen since he regularly explores that very theme in his own play. False reassurance by parents or childcare workers is a new casualty. It doesn't work anymore.

What keeps this fear manageable is the use of simple language to explain to him that "this Uncle Tommy is real, and the one you *thought* was Uncle Tommy is not, and of course you got scared, but you're OK now. That really *is* Uncle Tommy under there, and we'll show him to you so he won't scare you any more." This explanation of fact, combined with the parent's acceptance of the seriousness of the child's fear, reorganizes the child mentally so he can return to learning.

In all of this, however, don't forget that your little one does not see and experience the world the way you do. Not yet. Even when kids acquire more language, parents must not forget that the magic world is still there. Vacuum cleaners can persist as hungry monsters, and the bathtub drain may continue to be a source of real concern.

This is particularly worth remembering when your child is exploring. He may seem to be exploring like a scientist, but his imagination is still transforming what he observes. His version of "cause and effect" is probably not yours. I've seen two-year-olds work VCRs. I can only imagine why they think those pictures pop onto the TV screen! But I do know this: If a child displays uneasiness or fear in the face of a new "discovery," you should remember the

WORDS AND EMOTIONS

One remarkable use of combining explanation of fact with acceptance of emotion is in the psychotherapeutic techniques of clinicians who work with young children with emotional trauma and vulnerabilities.

For 20 years, I have been teaching an advanced seminar on the Inner Life of the Young Child at the Yale Child Study Center with my dear friend, psychoanalyst E. Kirsten Dahl. Together we have taught hundreds of advanced residents in child psychiatry and fellows in child psychology how to understand and work with young children and their families who suffer from mild to serious emotional and mental illness. Over and over, we help the young clinicians learn to identify in words what their young patients find upsetting or joyful as the children play and talk about the world they are living in and the relationships in that world.

Labeling their feelings and emotions not only helps them feel safer with what they are feeling so powerfully at an emotional level, it has another striking affect: *it organizes their behavior and their thinking at a more complex level.*

Here again we see the underappreciated critical link between emotion and learning, particularly as it is facilitated by play. This linkage works as well in healthy kids too, if not better, because healthy kids usually aren't struggling under complex emotional burdens.

This achievement can allow a child to express her emotions verbally rather than acting on them physically. How does the child go from acting mode to symbolic mode? She combines her maturing neurological capacities and her growing experience.

awesome power of the imagination, respect your child's emotional turmoil, and deal with it accordingly. And reassure, reassure, reassure.

In sum, play and imagination provide a powerful, effective way to cope with new fears in the child's expanding world. Imagination allows the child to be the master of past events and future unknowns, addressing his worries and working through them to a safe and happy ending.

EMOTION AND IMAGINATION

There is a clear progression in the way emotion and imagination link and support each other throughout toddlerhood. As emotions settle and are better controlled, the imagination has more room to grow. Both work together in building new foundations for social behavior. Take a look:

1. This era begins with increasing mood shifts and contrasts between states of feeling. It is not surprising to see a child move from compliant to stubborn in a manner of minutes. All this mood shifting has the effect of making him much more noticeable as a member of the family or community. It signals: "Sit up and take notice. I am very busy becoming *me*."

2. Next, having established the outer limits of his emotional domain, he begins to exert some control over the wide range of emotions he expresses, as though he has figured out that he'll get more of what he really needs (not to mention feel more comfortable) if he spends less time at the extremes of his emotional repertoire and more in the middle.

3. About this time, he begins to become more aware of the feelings of others, being less hectored by his own, and having achieved some self-regulation. At this point, Donny was able to share his beloved softie with his grandmother after she had stubbed her toe and sat down wincing in pain. Donny assumed, of course, that its magic would anesthetize Grandma as it did him.

4. This, in turn, allows him another observation about the social world around him: Cooperation has its benefits. Sharing allows for communal ownership of vast amounts of things he could not possibly control alone. Besides, adults are nuts about it.

5. Now that the waters are calmer, the sailing is easier and the discoveries start to pour in. The symbols of experience can now be used in play and learning. Fantasy play and pretend start to show up regularly in language.

6. Then, the child discovers she is not alone on these wonderful waters, and simple dramatic play themes with others emerge. We can play: "You baby, me mommy …" or "Let's go shopping…" or "Let's cook pancakes."

7. Finally, with all these wonderful new connections between emotion and play and learning, we arrive at a new level of awareness about fears. The dark, which had not been much of a problem before, now becomes full of trouble: monsters, bogeypersons, "saurs" (dino-).

The Role of Caregivers in Child's Play

The enrichment of learning by play, and vice versa, also holds for the quality of the child's relationships. Research tells us that kids who are securely attached to their caregivers are better players and hence, by our reasoning, better learners. Children who have received consistent high-quality care, both emotionally and physically, who are talked and listened to, and who have observed those around them involved in respectful interpersonal relationships carry their security — their self-confidence and feelings of self-worth — into play with others.

SIGNS OF EMOTIONALLY HEALTHY TODDLERS

During play, emotionally healthy kids show the following:

★They have richer fantasy lives than less-secure kids.

★They show a wide range of emotions, both positive and negative, when they play.

★They are adventuresome. They will tackle new experiences, and they are persistent and creative, yet flexible, as they explore and learn.

★They are confident around others. They stand up for themselves and won't put up with poor treatment from others. But they also show concern and empathy for other children and, at the right developmental stage, they are willing to share.

★They are optimistic in the face of problems or conflicts. Because of the care they have received, they have come to expect that things will turn out well.

Playing With Your Child

Now that you understand more of the many dimensions of play and imagination, you may better appreciate the importance and the opportunities of playing with your child. For example, the best way to know what your child thinks about his world before he can tell you directly in words is through playing with him. It is right there, in their play sequences and manipulations that we see and hear what they understand and think about the world we share.

Remember, however, that this is his play, not yours. You are a partner and a facilitator, occasionally a "go-fer," but you are not playwright, producer, or director.

PLAYING WITH YOUR CHILD

★ When you play make-believe with your child using simple dress-up (hats alone are great), narrate her play: "And now you get on your hat." Describe what you think she is feeling: "Don't you feel fancy (snazzy, cool…)!" And listen for when you are not quite on track: "So, then what?" Children often love to have you with them in these imaginary explorations of role and role-play and usually will do their best to keep you from getting lost along the way.

★ Use reflecting surfaces (mirrors, windows) as you play peekaboo with your child's image and then yours, or add a little face paint or make-up as he explores what happens to his face as he, or you, add a dot here or a line there. It helps him define who *he* is by enjoying the reflection of his face and feelings back and forth *between* you. Doing this together just feels different and better and usually more important.

★ Sit together in the dark with a flashlight and give your child a sense that he has some control over what appears, reappears, and disappears into the darkness. Narrate the experience with him, and match his level of emotional interest, as you share the job of turning the flashlight on and off together. Sara, at 22 months, loved this game and called it the "good-bye light game." She seemed to be sorting out the comings and goings of important things and people as the lights went off and on.

There are countless other ideas available from books and magazines. Borrow, invent, and reinvent games just for the two of you.

Even the simple game of put-and-take, probably the most ubiquitous game sequence in all of toddlerhood, is about the child learning how to make things appear, disappear, and reappear over and over and over. The simple reassurance that the toy *is* there again and again seems to comfort as it fascinates, preparing the child for the countless disappearances he faces in his life from this point forward.

Peekaboo is the interpersonal example of a similar, if more complex process. It is probably the most universal, transcultural game known to our species. It moves from the simple opening and closing of eyes, to removing a covering over the eyes, to turning around to find a voice not seen, to — when motor competence permits — crawling after the "lost" partner. Next, it is the child who is the "disappearer," as she initiates the sequence.

For example, a child might open the closet door and back into the dark, making intense eye contact with her invited pursuer. When eye contact is broken, she squeals with delight and waits 10 to 15 seconds in total silence before issuing a small grunt, as if to send a beacon of her whereabouts to her pursuer. She is the leaver in this sequence, and seems to savor the power inherent in the role. But, wait a second too long, and the teasing becomes abandonment fear, and the fun is over and the wailing starts. Toddlers have their limits, even when it's their game.

For this "play" to "work," language helps, but it is not essential. Memory, motor control, attachments to loving adults, symbolic thinking, and emotion all come together in this play to help children learn they are not alone. After words, it changes into hide-and-seek, and then cat-and-mouse, and then the game is afoot for the rest of one's life.

Joint play is so pleasurable to children this age. It is as though they are saying: "I feel so close to you, I want to keep it forever, especially when you are not here…." or "I need some reassurance that I'm okay when I can't see you." Yes, it's time-consuming, and there are not many shortcuts to this experience. But rest assured that their appetite for it is not perpetual, and before you know it, your child will prefer her peers to you, as is her destiny, and it is you who will feel a sting of loneliness when you lose your play buddy.

STYLES OF PLAY WITH MOMS AND DADS: VIVE LA DIFFERENCE!

One of my ongoing fields of study is the examination of the role of fathers in attachment and nurturing. What has my research revealed about how differently fathers play with children than mothers?

★ Fathers tend to engage in more physically stimulating play than mothers.

★ Not surprisingly, such interaction elicits more positive response from toddlers. This suggests that children seek out this type of behavior from fathers and the fathers, in turn, reinforce this behavior in their children. Fathers themselves tend to find greater satisfaction in more active rather than passive pursuits with their young children, so it is mutually gratifying.

★ Dads seem to have a penchant for making even the mundane routines more physical, whether its pushing a stroller or giving a bath.

★ In verbal and non-verbal communication, fathers use shorter, staccato-like bursts of language and physical stimulation, while mothers are more modulated and predictable.

Despite the patterns, researchers have found only minimal gender-typing from such play. Henry Lytton of the University of Michigan found that although father interaction with children encourages gender-typed activities, such as play with gender-typed toys or games, their influence was quite small. Furthermore, any trends favoring parental sex difference in interaction style diminished with age.

The Arts in Play, Learning, and Imagination

We cannot possibly end our chapter without a brief discussion of the role of the arts in play, learning, imagination, and feeling.

Visual arts: Between 18 and 36 months, most little ones have magic marker mania because kids are driven to make images. Give him plenty of markers or crayons and plenty of paper. Let him scribble away (on both sides). Let him do it his way. Allow him to turn the scribble into whatever. Don't mess with it, impose structure on it, or repeatedly ask what it is. All these intrusions run the risk of teaching the child he is supposed to be doing something other than what he is attempting to do. His ideas are better than yours precisely because they are *his,* not yours.

It's an important developmental stage. Here, the physical process of tuning fine-motor skills becomes a learning experience about texture, shapes, color, etc. This starts a process which eventually involves symbolic use and manipulation of images. It just *looks* like mud wrestling.

As they paint, scribble, push, and knead clay or work with other materials, they chat, they narrate, they improve eye-hand coordination, and may become involved in group efforts. Later on you can work with "inside the lines," and " Make it look like…" And don't forget to have them help you clean up after they are through. That's a good lesson in shared work, accomplishment, and restoring order.

Music (and, not coincidentally, dance): Children have an innate appetite for music. Music is the superb para-language between emotion, expression, and imagination. Here in the musical world, feelings come together with play, movement, and memory in a way that is not ultimately dependent on language. And that is precisely why it is so indispensable to the young child across culture and class.

All young children, even those with only minimal hearing, have a powerful, almost riveting affinity for music. Research has shown that the fetus responds to musical cues from the middle trimester onward and never stops attending to it afterward. And infants are the same. Watch an infant's face as you sing or play music. Even words rarely elicit such a complex reaction. The desire to move and bounce to, kick feet to, rock back and forth to — even match the mood of — almost any musical stimulus is powerful in most children.

By the era we are discussing, play with music is so complex and rich, it probably teaches more economically than any formal kind of instruction. The neurobiological processes underlying the appreciation and facilitation of music-assisted play and interaction involve the brain pathways for memory, hearing, balance, motor control, hormonal secretion, cognition, and, of course, emotion. Talk about a big bang for the developmental buck!

Take the simple circle song "…all fall down" (I grew up with the version "Ashes, ashes, we all fall down," at which point everyone collapses to the ground while still trying to hold hands). What is the expression on the child's face as he anticipates the collapse, knowing exactly what is about to happen, evoked repeatedly by the senseless musical cue? What role does cooperation play? Motoric competence? Interpersonal interest? Memory? Emotion? Shared emotion? Imagination? Which element is primary? What else in our world can stir such a mutual response across generations and cultures? I can't think of a thing.

The Road Traveled in These 18 Months

By now, it should be clear that the importance of play to learning and imagination during this period can't be exaggerated. Nor can the scope of a child's development at this time.

Somewhere between 18 to 36 months, one of the most important world-altering discoveries made by children is that one thing can stand for another. An image can represent an experience and so can a word, just as a word can now represent a thing. The ability to symbolize leads a child from the world of behavior to the world of ideas. It also helps her to express her own emotions and her experience of her inner self, and to connect, through imagination, with the feelings, desires, and experiences of others.

It is in this developmental era that the growth in the child's ability to express emotion finally permits her, through her play and learning, to achieve more complex and interesting levels of understanding the world. The increasing maturity of her emotional self sets the stage for greater social learning and the resulting growth in personality and cooperation that will get her ready for the demands of childcare in a group setting. It is remarkable to see how this fits together. It is truly a wonder. Enjoy! ★

GROWNUP PLAY

A wonderful way to play with and teach your child is to bring her into *your* world. Toys are great, but they are no substitute for real contributions to the grown-up world where the real things of life happen. It's in this grown-up world that children come to see themselves as players, not bench warmers. And when they contribute what they can to that world, self-esteem gets a big boost.

Have your child help with your chores. Involve her in whatever way you can with your work. Include her in your hobbies and favorite pastimes as well. Children love to do "grown-up" things, and to imitate others. When you let them work and play alongside you, they get the best of both worlds.

Work-as-play: Bring your child into the household routine. There are countless safe ways for a young child to "help" with meals, laundry, shopping, cleaning, and washing the car. He will learn skills and know that he is integral to the household's functioning. Yes, the chores will take longer as your child learns the ropes, makes mistakes, and works at a snail's pace, but the value to his learning and his self-regard are more than worth the extra time.

Find ways to involve your child in your work. One thing sacrificed in today's work world is children's participation — where they learn and are valued — in the family business. Not so a generation or two ago when far more children stacked cans at Mom and Pop's grocery, or sorted materials at the family tailor shop. Self-esteem was less of a problem for those kids. They knew the family business, in some small but valued way, depended on them, too. Many of today's kids are not involved at all in family work, and may not even know or understand what their parents do for a living. "Work" is some shadowy thing that happens when Mom and Dad aren't at home, or is even something that keeps parents from being home. No wonder such parents get a blank look from their child when they try to explain they had a hard day at the office. What's an office?

Hobbies and pastimes: Share your interests with your child. It's important for parents to keep up with their own passions. You need "a life," and you won't have one if you lose yourself totally in your child's world. Keep up with the piano, chess, painting, hiking, letter writing, whatever. Teach your child about your avocations. Let her be a part of what you love. This is one of the most intriguing, emotionally rich forms of learning children get. And you are building a common bond that will last for years.

CHAPTER 8

Limits and Affection

The power of relationships in shaping a child's behavior and sense of self.
When to make a deal, and when to cut your losses.
What about spoiling?

Discipline is such a versatile word. It can mean behavior or an academic category (the "discipline" of law or divinity). Its oldest meaning, however, is traced back to the word for "teach," and boy, is that a good thing to remember whenever you are concerned about setting limits on your little one's behavior. Because above all, you are teaching her by *your* behavior how she should eventually handle *hers.*

Whatever it means to you as a parent, discipline doesn't mean much at the start of this era, but usually means way too much by the end. The reason: the child's discovery of the power his own impulses have over himself and others. In this chapter, we will examine how to help you and your young child understand and feel safe with each other's impulses by exploring what they mean and how they can be controlled.

Children at this age actually don't drive everyone nuts. Some people think they are absolutely adorable. But the trouble comes when they figure out how to drive you nuts, can't stop, and you are not amused. Negotiating, caving in, cutting deals, bribing, physical removal, using your wits, and begging all have their place. Physical punishment and not keeping your word do not.

We also will discuss the great significance of a child's developing ability to feel shame and its surprising importance to future development. Spoiling and spanking get discussed and debated. Finally, we'll look at the special challenges of our times — parents who work or are divorced or separated — and how these circumstances often affect the way a parent deals with limits.

One priceless maxim reminds us that discipline belongs in the domain of affection and respect: *"Do unto others as you would have them do unto others."*

New Tests for Parents

The tremendous growth during this 18- to 36-month period puts increasing pressure on the child to become more powerful in achieving her ends, get what she wants, and get it now. Dogged determination comes into play. So does negativism. A robust "No!" is the most basic expression of independence — the simplest assertion of self.

Often for the first time, parents find themselves in a terrible bind when their wonderful new love for their increasingly autonomous toddler is put to the test. Most of us are caught off guard with this development. We are surprised by the tenacity of our young ones to push our buttons and take us to the limit over and over again. We forget that negativism and limit-testing are trying for us, but they are very enjoyable for the child. She is changing from a passive recipient to an active participant in our world. In fact, clinicians worry if negativism *doesn't* show up.

Nonetheless, it's very tempting for parents to try to "nice" their children out of this challenging behavior with sweet talk and cajoling. Unfortunately, this doesn't work in the short term, and it defeats our purpose of shaping a child's behavior positively in the long term. Moreover, kids see through it in a heartbeat. Then they've really got your number!

"Phony" just doesn't work with kids. Real, honest emotion, however, works wonders. When you connect with your child's frustration or anger, you open a constructive path for coping with such emotions. When your child sees and *feels* your disappointment or upset — appropriately displayed — he has a better chance to understand the effect his actions have produced. This is central to teaching him what kind of behavior is acceptable and what is not. Moreover, he learns that it's OK to feel what he's feeling and express those emotions appropriately — another invaluable lesson.

Keeping Sight of the Goal

So much happens in the behavior and discipline arena during this 18-month period that it's easy to lose sight of the objective. The long-term goal here is *self-control* in the child, *not parental control* of the child. You are teaching the basics of judgment and control that will work, not only when you are around to enforce the rules, but later on, when you aren't. Comes in very handy during those pesky teen years.

This period starts out with a child's budding sense of shame — remorse *after* the fact. If you manage the next 18 months well, the end products are the basics of self-control — an understanding of consequences *before* an act, and the ability and willingness to refrain from that act. This self-control is the cornerstone of conscience.

A conscience as grownups know it doesn't begin to take shape until around five or six years of age. It will take years to reach its full state at the onset of adulthood, but the foundation is being laid now.

Conscience and self-control cannot develop on their own. Both must be taught — by example, by patient teaching, and by consistently enforcing age-appropriate limits. Because of the way the brain, mind, and all facets of a child's personality grow and intertwine from 18 to 36 months, teaching is easiest and most effective in this period — even though it may not always look that way.

The Importance of Limits

Limits define where a child's world, safety, and autonomy begin and end. When these limits are clear, a child is free to go on to more interesting and valuable activities — like discovery and learning. Children will continually retest boundaries, just to make sure they're in good working order. But if the limits stay firm, retesting will become less frequent and more manageable.

As your child seeks to win your approval and to find the boundaries in her world, the easier you make her search, the better for both of you because of the wonderful results:

> ★ *Acceptable behavior:* **A winsome child is miles ahead of the perpetually demanding whiner. It's fun being around pleasant kids for children and adults alike.**

★ *Learning:* **Children who continually test or search for boundaries (either because those boundaries keep shifting or don't exist) have *less* time and energy for the really important work – exploration, discovery, and learning.**

★ *Intellectual development:* **To think through a planned action and its consequences — Will something break? Will Mommy be unhappy? — is an important achievement for toddlers. It builds cognitive capacities just as surely as thinking through and resolving any other problem. Children need this formative experience, and without consistent limits, they won't get it.**

A good example of how important it is to provide limits is clearly shown by Sean and his parents.

The Daredevil

At 22 months old, Sean seemed fearless. At the park, he ran after any dog within range, regardless of size or leash. He would fling himself into any activity, be it down a darkened basement stairs or off the edge of a swimming pool. Headlong, he careened down supermarket or shopping mall aisles, daring his huffing and puffing parents to rein him in. Laughing and giggling, he gave his parents the impression that he was having one terrific time.

It was hard for his folks to deny him this "pleasure." They had both come from unhappy homes and were afraid that some effects of their childhoods – fighting, yelling, and being from economically unstable families – would "rub off on him and make him feel like a loser."

His young parents loved but feared him. They couldn't see what he really needed because they wanted to assure themselves that he would not suffer life's terrors the way they had. Although all the hearts were in the right place, ideas about who they were to each other were not. Sean was struggling to find a safe balance between his innate drive to explore the fascinations of the world about him with his innate need to feel securely attached to his parents. More than freedom, what he really needed was an occasionally firm, "No, Sean, running wild is just going to scare you. I'll hold your hand till you're settled down."

Charles Zeanah's work on attachment, at Tulane, reminds us that there is clearly a biological propensity for children to attach to preferred nurturing figures in their lives for security. By the age we are discussing, children should have long since established their faith in a "secure base." In fact, it is highly unlikely that a child by 18 months old or older will feel securely attached to any figure who can not keep them safe and protected.

That is why we came to understand Sean's recklessness as coping behavior. It actually served as a solution to a big problem for him, dangerous though it was. He was constantly testing the proposition, "How far can I go to feel secure in their love of me?" And he desperately needed to know the answer, or he'd go on testing himself and the people he'd meet for the rest of his life. This is why limits are so essential for a child's happiness and healthy development.

By age three, children are still pretty much pleasure-seekers. But with the right guidance, they should have a good grounding in the boundaries of their world and your expectations of them. Lapses will be frequent, but that's expected.

Building Self-Control and Conscience

Of course, limits provide much more than security for a child. They are essential to the long-term process of building a conscience.

An Act of Contrition

Eli, age 26 months, sat quietly at the table as his father prepared his dinner, placing the macaroni and cheese with strawberries and a chicken nugget on his favorite plate. Eli was hungry, but exhausted, having had a fun-packed day with his older cousin. His Dad affectionately smoothed his hair as he laid the dish in front of his son, and Eli promptly screamed, "Stupid food! No!" If his father had been any slower removing the plate, its contents would be oozing slowly down the wall.

Yes, Eli had entered the phase of the picky eater just weeks before. But the problem remains of how to respond to Eli's shot across Dad's bow.

To Dad's amazement, as he was silently collecting his thoughts about how to respond, Eli shocked him by crunching up a contrite face saying softly, "Sorry, Daddy." Dad could not have been more surprised.

The only way to explain this scene is by understanding the timely arrival of a highly complex feeling in this toddler — shame. It changes everything, usually for the better, because now the parent has an *internal* ally in her struggle to help the child develop inner control over his impulses. What makes its arrival so interesting is that, like most developmental milestones — walking, talking, etc. — one day it simply appears.

But as we have learned before in this book, it does not come out of nowhere. Building blocks have been laid as the child has begun to learn to control his wild mood swings. Research reassures us that children make big strides in self-control during this period. By 18 months children can follow one or two clear and simple commands. This gives them more faith in cause-and-effect. By 36 months, the control mechanism can mature incredibly, given the right encouragement.

PICKY EATING

Picky eating is a common worry spot for parents who remember their little bouncer doubling his weight by birthday number one (completely normal). But toddlers need only gain a fraction of that, usually three to five pounds during the year, and the reduction in rate of appetite increase sometimes worries parents. The appearance at about the same time of the word "no" makes the food domain a coliseum ripe for conflict. Small portions of old favorites and new specials, presented interestingly but with a touch of parental disinterest, bolstered by a yogurt or salad dressing dip, is usually enough to weather this temporary, developmental storm.

For many years scientists debated whether shame, pride, and guilt emerge simultaneously or in sequence. Research shows that there is, in fact, an orderly sequence, one that makes a lot of sense. For clarity, let's work with some basic definitions:

- ★ *Embarrassment:* **Feeling self-conscious or flustered**
- ★ *Shame:* **Feeling that one has lost the respect of others**
- ★ *Guilt:* **Feeling that one deserves punishment**

The pattern of how these attributes gel suggests a logical order to the shaping of behavior and to the limit-setting techniques that will work best during this period. It's important to understand what a child can and cannot understand and do at each stage. That way you won't expect too much — or too little — at any given point. You also won't use tactics that your child cannot understand or that are likely to backfire.

THE PATH TO SELF-CONTROL AND CONSCIENCE

14 Months
★ Manifestation of embarrassment.

18 Months
★ Child begins to follow simple directions (two- to three-word instructions).
★ Manifestation of discovery of self and the drive to exert autonomy:
  - rise of negativism
  - onset of the child's desire to do things her way and by herself.
★ Early signs of shame.

24 Months
★ Reasoning and memory increase and reinforce one another.
★ Growing development of shame.
★ Child begins to learn limits, to understand the implications of breaking them, and to appreciate reinforcement techniques.

30 Months
★ Early signs of guilt as the child comes to expect punishment for breaking important rules.
★ Child may show strong emotion, yelling, even screaming "Sorry, Mommy" after some minor infraction, trying to head off too much disappointment or to shorten the time shame is felt.

36 Months
★ Child's ability to follow simple directions from others begins to grow into an ability to direct her own behavior.
★ Growing control over emotions, particularly frustration and anger. A 36-month-old will be able to cope with many events or circumstances that would have overwhelmed him 18 months earlier.
★ *Onset of growing self-control and emerging sense of right and wrong — the basic elements of conscience.*

Five to Six Years
★ Emergence of conscience as child is able to combine the sense of right and wrong with self-control.

End of Adolescence
★ Fully developed conscience.

As you can see, this is an incredibly important time in a child's life — one in which the emotions, language, reason, trust, and control come together in a way that lets you shape a solid foundation for your child's behavior from then on.

The "Science" of Shame and the Evolution of Conscience

The joy of discovery increasingly compels a child into more independent exploration. The drive to learn begins to compensate for being left on his own while he's learning. If play and learning have been fun up to this point, a child will feel safe and be happy venturing further from his parents for longer periods of time when he is immersed in new learning. The child's growing exploits in pursuit of learning lead to the requirement for limits. From the child's viewpoint, his exploits offer wonderful opportunities to test those limits.

The shaping of behavior during this period is made possible by the continuing surge of brain development. Throughout this 18 months, the brain will become increasingly complex in its capacity to link emotion and thought and to regulate emotional events.

At the beginning of the period, neural connections exist between the cortex (the outer muscle and sensory parts of the brain) and the inner hypothalamus (the center for the autonomic, or "automatic," reflexive parts of the brain). Many of these "experience-dependent" parts of the brain have now had enough experiences (we hope good ones, as opposed to neglectful or traumatic ones, which are also brain-growing experiences) to shape brain architecture in a beneficial way. If this brain-growing has been good, a child may already be able to modulate intense emotions, such as rage, without extensive conscious thought.

If caregiving experiences have built a reasonable level of trust, the toddler can now build on that trust and begin honing rage protests into useful forms of power and energy, like the drive to be competent and assertive. This, in turn, fuels growing autonomy.

Also, thanks to these new brain connections, distress-relieving mechanisms begin to function more automatically. The child is easier to comfort, both on his own and with the help of others. Drawing on memory, he can call up a comforting "picture" of a loved object or person to help soothe himself when distress or frustration starts. He also can modulate negative emotions enough to go snuggle with Mom or Dad, instead of raging that they did not appear the instant he wanted.

On top of these advances, his vocabulary is growing fast, which allows a whole new avenue for expressing and understanding feelings — words like "good" and "bad," " yes" and "no."

All of these elements work together to create an environment in which limit-setting is possible and highly effective.

Toddlers first begin to feel embarrassment and then shame as a reaction when their behavior falls short of *external* standards — primarily those set by parents.

Guilt is the next step on the teaching ladder. With consistent reinforcement, children begin to *internalize* their parents' standards for expected behavior, and adopt those standards. They also come to know the consequences of breaking the rules, and they come to expect those consequences. Voilá — guilt. The ability to expect consequences is another critical stone in the foundation of conscience.

Children first test, then internalize the limits you set. This is the product of growing self-control. It's not uncommon to see a child, who has repeatedly been told not to touch a forbidden object, approach that object, stop, say "no touch," and then walk away. She may practice this routine many times as she comes to own the limit and make it hers, not just her parents'.

The work of Allan Schore has revolutionized the way we think about this progression. The implications of his work for a child's capacity for internal behavioral control and emotional and moral development are staggering.

Dr. Schore's exceptional contribution has been to suggest that *shame helps the brain to "wire up" in a way that allows self-control to develop* in the child.

Shame allows, and possibly stimulates, further growth in the parts of the brain having to do with reasoning, moral development, memory and emotion. Of course, too little or too much shame can under- or overshoot the mark. But some is apparently essential.

Shame arises when a toddler gets an unexpectedly negative reaction from someone else. A disapproving response from a parent is all the more powerful when it is not expected. For the toddler, the experience is that of deflation — a big "comedown" from her normal "Aren't I terrific!" ebullience. Deflation brings with it the physical signs we see in others (and see and feel in ourselves, too) — the drooped head, the hang-dog look, maybe even a blush.

The capacity for shame comes about as the brain — especially its "thinking" and "feeling" components — continues to grow and mature. At the same time, the child's experiences, including shame, affect the way that brain growth occurs.

According to Dr. Schore, shame changes the child's behavior over time, not just as the child "learns" what actions cause a parent's displeasure, but by causing brain development that allows that behavior to change. The central nervous system actually develops new circuits that are essential for further social and emotional growth, not to mention body mastery. (Bladder and bowel control, for example, grow right alongside control of aggressive impulses.)

This goes to the heart of why limit-setting at this stage is so important. The rapid growth of the brain up to the age of three is an incredible help in getting a child's behavior off on the right foot.

A Practical Guide to Setting Limits

The tired old adage, "practice makes perfect," is a cornerstone of teaching acceptable, responsible behavior to a child. Limit-setting for about the first two years of life rests on you — specifically on your ability to distract and, if needed, remove your child to ensure safety and socially acceptable behavior.

These actions (plus child-proofing the premises as much as possible) have been shown over and over to be the most effective ways to keep behavior in check without quashing a toddler's delight in exploring and learning.

What is being taught in distraction and removal (along with a firm "no") are patterns of what's acceptable and what's not. When your actions are consistent, each repetition sinks a little deeper into the well of your child's memory. This happens even before his cognitive powers are up to the task of understanding the whys of safety rules or of more complex concepts, such as value and ownership, which govern what he can and can't do with objects.

TEMPERAMENTAL FIT BETWEEN PARENT AND CHILD

It is good to remind ourselves that our children are developing in very close proximity to us and to our own capacities to feel shame and invoke our consciences in useful, constructive ways. It will help to take a brief look at our own styles and think about how they will affect our children at this age.

The temperamental "fit" between parent and child plays a big role in the limit-setting process. If this process is to work well, the challenge is to keep drawing your child toward greater and greater self-control.

The fit or match between your style and that of your toddler will never be perfect, nor should it be. However, thinking about how you affect each other can greatly increase the ease with which you set limits for her and help her stay in control when she is threatening to "lose it."

When you are well tuned to your child, both of you are likely to feel more in control. As a result, your child doesn't have to resort to ever more dramatic tactics, like shutting down completely or running away.

By the same token, repeated misreading of what a child needs in the limit-setting realm, coupled with too little or too much discipline, leaves her feeling confused and that she has failed as a communicator. These feelings, in turn, lead to a sense of uselessness and hopelessness. So it's a good idea to periodically reassess your style and that of your child to see where differences could be helpful or troublesome.

The first sign of memory related to limits is when you see your child looking over his shoulder as he moves toward some forbidden object. You probably noticed some of these "catch me if you can" grins and challenges to your "noes" back when your child was just crawling. You also have probably experienced many a bout when your child has dissolved into tears after spilling or breaking something. Herein lie the seeds of shame — healthy shame, the kind that regrets an error or mistake. And, yes, there is a conflict. Your child's desire to please you at this stage runs right into his need to figure out the boundaries in his world.

Fortunately, the solution to both sides of the conflict is the same — consistency on your part in maintaining the rules. *Consistent repetitions of the same words and acts by you enable your child to begin to feel embarrassment and shame when she breaks the rules.* This is a very healthy development, one that is central to her ability to control her own behavior in the future, when you are not around to act as policeman. If this process goes as it should, *by 36 months your child will show the beginnings of self-control as well as the first signs of a sense of right and wrong. These are the foundations of conscience.*

Unlike physical skills, such as walking, a conscience doesn't emerge on its own. It is a product of parental guidance and teaching, and its early signs are clear markers that you are getting the job done.

Key to your success is your child's desire to please you. These are important assets for you to use in this 18-month period. The process is slow and time-consuming, but in the long run more than worth the investment of your patience, time, and effort. This is when your approval is a powerful tool to coax a child to verbalize her wants and needs rather than to act out her emotions. Conversely, withholding your approval and/or showing disapproval are strong motivators for little ones to stop unacceptable behavior.

Growing language and memory skills increasingly allow a child to remember a past rule-breaking event, how he felt about it, and what happened. Over time, these remembrances can get called up earlier and more easily when temptation beckons. This sets the stage for controlling the impulse, not breaking the rule.

"Will I Spoil My Child?"

No discussion of limits would be complete without addressing spoiling. First, it's helpful to look at just what we mean by "spoiling." Most adults believe a spoiled child is one who behaves in a way that the adult finds objectionable. But what's "objectionable?" The answer varies widely among cultures and individuals.

It's a Tough World

In the years that I have been evaluating and treating young children and their families at the inner-city child development clinic run by the Yale Child Study in New Haven, I have seen many thoughtful and loving young African-American and Latino mothers and fathers being "a little rough," as one grandmother described it, with their young children when setting limits. I had no doubt the children were deeply loved, so this was a perpetual surprise to me. It seemed out of step with the way these parents comforted, taught, played with, and fed their kids.

Finally, I asked one of the mothers about my observation and she said, yes, she was very aware that she was doing it. "It's my way of getting him ready for the life out there in the world, where it's tough and rough. It makes no sense to pretend to him that the world cares about him the way I do, so I am very careful not to spoil him when he steps over the line. The parents that spoil their kids are setting them up for a long, hard fall." OK.

Too Much of a Good Thing

On a recent visit to China, my wife and I saw another cultural variation on the spoiling theme. This one fascinated and worried us. In Xi'an we visited a kindergarten which cared for more than 100 children five days a week. The majority of the children boarded Monday through Friday. The caregivers were loving and well-respected by the community, but they and their principal were starved for advice about how to deal with the dramatic increase in the number of unruly, ill-mannered, swearing, disrespectful preschool children who did not respond to the usual discipline or reprimands.

As we listened, it became clear that the teachers were very concerned that all these problem children were misbehaving as a result of having been "spoiled" by being treated like "little emperors" in families of six adults (parents and maternal and paternal grandparents) to only one child – a by-product of China's policy of one child per family. The implications of the "little emperor" syndrome were worrisome, and we are working with others to assess how widespread such problems are and what can be done to ameliorate them in a culturally competent and sensitive manner.

As these examples show, what's important to one person can be irrelevant to the next, what's cute to one can be bothersome to another. In our multicultural society, the key is for you, others in your home, and those who care for your child to agree on the basics.

Once those basics are set, reason and consistency are your best tactics. Giving in from time to time won't ruin your rules or spoil your child. If something is really important to the little guy, let him win on occasion (except where safety and minimal behavior requirements are concerned). It shows him that his views have merit and teaches him that perseverance on things that really count for him can be rewarded. Especially give in on those instances where your initial position was extreme or unnecessary — something all adults do from time to time, even with other adults.

If caving becomes a habit, however, you do no one a favor, least of all your child. The boundaries she needs to feel secure get muddied, and she will spend untold effort to reestablish them — a big waste of resources for her and a big test of your patience.

Within the limits you set there is never a need for limits on your love. Care and affection don't spoil a child. In fact, they provide the best teaching model a child could ask for. You are demonstrating the very behavior you want to encourage. There is no downside to this.

The Annoyances of Toddler Behavior

A lot of a child's behavior that adults may find annoying is not only normal, it's beneficial to a child's growth. Endless repetition of anything and everything falls near the top of many adults' "least favorite" lists. But repetition is how children learn. That their repeated action produces the same outcome teaches children about the physical universe and gives them a healthy sense of control because they learn how to produce a desired effect.

Non-stop touching and exploration also can be annoying. But these behaviors, too, are essential to learning.

Saying "no" is another common marker of the period. It is part quest for limits and part assertion of autonomy.

Fortunately, the duration of these learning tactics is mercifully brief. With patience and ingenuity on your part, all parties can come through unscathed, and limit-setting can be aimed at the big issues where it really counts — safety and good behavior.

TO SPANK OR NOT TO SPANK

My strong advice is no. Dr. Schore's findings may be the best reason for avoiding violence of any type. His work shows the longlasting value of shame in building self-control. When this powerful emotion sets in after wrongdoing, you want to work with it, not interrupt it. If physical punishment gets tossed into the mix, it brings a host of new emotions into play — most commonly fear and anger — and shame gets crowded out or short-circuited.

As I noted earlier, the goal in discipline is the child's control of himself, not the parent's control of the child. The latter doesn't work so well when the parent is not around (or isn't looking).

A study by the American Academy of Pediatrics also shows the downside of physical punishment: Children in the study who were regularly spanked turned out to be less controlled and more prone to confrontational behavior in school. Ah, the power of parental example. Furthermore, the child learns to fear and avoid the parent, not the bad behavior.

In my years in the consulting room, it has gradually dawned on me that most spanking is a parental temper tantrum. You can't teach children to gain control of their impulses by losing yours.

Unfortunately, there hasn't been all that much research on discipline and the effects of differing disciplinary practices. However, the anecdotal evidence for the value of non-violent tactics is strong and consistent, and my observations in 25 years as a clinician bear this out. In the absence of findings to the contrary, it just makes sense to give children the advantages that non-violence is continually shown to produce.

Sometimes Limits Are Hard to Maintain

Despite the importance of limits, parents sometimes have trouble setting and maintaining them. Part of the problem stems, no doubt, from the changes in today's family structures and lifestyles. Some common issues:

⭐ *I don't want to be the ogre:* Parents who are unable to spend much time with their children (because of work, separation, or divorce, for example) may be concerned about how they are viewed by their children in the limited time they have together. Anxious not to be the "Wicked Witch of the West," they cave easily and often. But children are relentless in their search for limits since, at this age, they can't set their own. The result of the caving is more testing, rather than less. Better an occasional stand-your-ground action than a non-stop war of attrition. With limits, children — and the limited time parents have with them — will be much happier. The bonds between parent and child also will be stronger.

⭐ *I'm too tired:* This is a common problem of working parents. They come home after a long day, looking forward to some pleasant time with the family, and, boom, they get hit with whines or cries. Caving again may seem the quickest route to peace. And, in the short term, it might be. But it only increases the frequency of testing. Once again, standing firm for important limits will make those pleasant evenings the norm, not the exception.

⭐ *Giving in is a treat for the child:* It isn't. It's downright scary. Freedom in life is a treat for us growups because we have, in general, mastered the self-control needed to use it properly. A toddler hasn't. Limits are the controls that make his life safe, secure, and happy. Don't deny him these essentials.

The Basics of Setting Limits

So how do you maintain limits? For the most part, your disapproval is a stronger deterrent than you may appreciate, at least during these first three years. But for disapproval to be effective, your child will need to learn that your frown is only the "first string" and that you have "bench strength." This is where reward and punishment come in.

First, on a positive note, one of the strongest elements in maintaining limits is to reward good behavior. Your approval and support mean the world to a toddler looking to you for a smile. The more time your child spends seeking — and getting — your approval for the right things, the less time he will spend on the wrong things.

However, the wrong things will happen. It's an inevitable part of how children learn. No doubt you already have been amazed at what a master your little one can be. It often seems that children can home in on a hot button or weak moment with laser-like precision. The annoying part is that, to them, this all seems like fun. And it is. Learning how "buttons" on people work is just as fascinating a discovery — and just as important — as learning how buttons on a toy work. For us, however, it's another matter.

The Un-Birthday Girl

Reilly was 32 months when her little brother had his first birthday party. Her mom and dad had anticipated trouble from "the greenies," (their word for Reilly's jealously and envy), and had asked grandparents to be on the lookout and maybe bring a sibling gift to ease the pain. They had done all the right things, making Reilly a part of the celebration, giving her the "special birthday sister chair," asking her to help with the cupcakes, etc., sandbagging ahead of time for trouble.

Nevertheless, Reilly reached her limit somewhere after the sixth or seventh present was opened. She angled over near her brother's chair and pushed it over, spilling him unceremoniously into his pile of newly opened gifts. She seemed surprised at the group's disapproval, seemingly thinking it would be understandable behavior, given the outrageous amount of attention her brother was receiving.

Her mother firmly and quietly escorted her off the stage as her father comforted her startled brother, taking her daughter to her room with a simple, "I guess you've had enough." (She wisely ignored the disdainful comments of assembled family members – she is the mother, thank you, and she knows her child.)

First, she let herself calm down, and second, she said to her silent, pouting daughter, "I know this has been hard to see your brother get all this attention" (validating what Reilly was probably feeling).

Then some silence as Reilly softens and looks at her mother for the first time.

Third, she asked her daughter, "How were you feeling before you pushed Sam over?" and she waits a long time for a response, but she expects one nonetheless.

Eventually, a head-bowed, barely audible, but very heartfelt, "I want more presents, too." Mom acknowledges the wish as OK and perfectly understandable, and her day will come again.

She lays down the law yet again about using words instead of hurting the people you love and then asks finally, "What should we do now to make this better?" Reilly crawls up into her lap and after a brief cry says she wants to give Sam the sibling present she got from Grandma and Grandpa.

Patience, calm, and firmness from Mom. Shame, reflection, and repairing the breach from Reilly. (Important to the mix: Mom is confident in her approach, and not swayed by the "helpful advice" from well-meaning friends and relatives.)

A Budding Picasso

At 30 months, my nephew Ben loved to paint, color and draw. Looking for new venues in which to ply his talent, he spied the prized family Bible. In just moments, five generations of recorded family history were illuminated by an affectionate, exuberant splash of crayon color.

An intentional act of wanton destruction? In this case, no. Ben knew how the family valued that Bible and he naturally wanted to be included in it. What better way than to use his new creative skills, which had previously always been greeted with smiles and praise by his parents?

Understanding motivation or intent when your toddler/preschooler does something unacceptable can help relieve your anger and frustration and open the door to a more constructive reaction. The best response in this case would be teaching, not punishment. That, plus keeping valuables out of the child's reach and the art supplies in use only under supervision.

BASIC POINTERS FOR SETTING LIMITS

Be a role model. Children this age are highly imitative and like to please. The more good behavior you demonstrate, the more they will copy. The more approval they get for their good behavior, the more good behavior you will get from them.

Keep rules to a minimum. Focus on the big-ticket items that govern safety and the important aspects of social behavior. To set more rules than your child can manage at any given age is just confusing.

Be consistent. Enforce rules consistently. Only set rules you will maintain.

Don't overreact. Children explore behavior in stages. When a new behavior emerges that is unacceptable, such as biting or using bad language, overreaction on your part can actually reinforce it. Kids like oversized reactions. Moreover, they remember what really gets your goat — those actions come in very handy when you're near the breaking point. So don't tip your hand. A firm "we don't bite," followed by removal, if necessary, is much better than a big flap. On bigger issues, such as stealing (not uncommon before children understand the concept of ownership), calm explanations work best.

Match punishment to the child's understanding. Don't use punishment until a child is cognitively capable of understanding what action is being punished and why. Children don't reach this level of mental maturity until somewhere near the second birthday. Punishment before this achievement is just confusing to a child. If tendered on a regular basis, a child can withdraw from the entire category of activities that include the offense. As a result, he may curtail exploration that is essential to learning. Until a child can understand the offense, parents should use distraction and physical removal to stop unwanted or unsafe behavior.

Punishment should be effective. When your tactics aren't working, reassess. As your child's language skills improve, you can involve her in the process. Ask what would help her improve her control next time, and what you should do if she doesn't exercise that control. Loads of research shows that corporal punishment is less effective over the long term than tactics such as timeouts. Moreover, it teaches the wrong lesson — that violence and physical control are the ways to resolve differences.

Punishment should be appropriate. Punishment should fit the child's stage of development, temperament, and "crime." Don't overdo. Especially in the early years, keep punishment for the major infractions, especially those involving safety. Don't waste big ammunition on small stuff. It cheapens the currency and weakens its effectiveness.

Match your behavior to the outcome you want. The way that you act when you set a limit matters as much as your technical prowess in carrying through. Sometimes, your child is so relieved at your calm, you don't even have to carry through.

Provide clear expectations followed by anything that encourages self-control. Use words: "Biting means you have to be away from us for awhile." Anything that helps a child feel in charge of his impulses, even briefly, is money in the self-control (and self-esteem) bank. Being the boss of one's body or temper is the eventual goal, and language can help your child understand what you and he are trying to work out together.

Fathers and Discipline

As you've noticed, the majority of examples in the book depict children interacting with their mothers, and that statistically remains predominately true. But census data show that fathers are more involved with their children than ever before in this century, and that trend is likely to continue, given women's continued movement into the work force. Most of the advice regarding limits fits fathers as well as it does mothers. As you will see in the next chapter, disciplining a child of the same sex feels different to men and women, with some interesting results.

The one area where a father's discipline tends to differ from a mother's is in the "why" of discipline. Although this difference is less important for younger children than for school-age kids, it's worth introducing here for you first-time parents to help you appreciate the importance of having *both* parents participate in limit-setting and discipline. It turns out to be a real advantage to child and parent.

MANAGING AN INFRACTION

Keep it short and simple. About six to eight words is the upper limit here, and don't repeat it endlessly, as it means less every time you say it.

Move in sooner rather than later as the excitement of the act itself starts to take over and the child can no longer hear what she might have heard a minute or two before. Don't give more than two warnings before you move in to resolve the situation.

Use your words, not your hands.

Stop kicking the door.

Label the child's feeling or wish: "I know it's so hard to wait," or "That made you so angry."

Follow with what you expect: "We don't hurt people here," or "Screaming won't help me know what you need," or "I will help you calm down."

Conclude with a solution, joint when possible: "Is book time a good idea?" or "Would 'softie' help you settle down?" or "How can we fix this?"

Always remember to count to 10. It actually works.

If needed, punishment tactics that have proven their worth over the years are:

★ Timeouts
★ Physical removal
★ Immobilization (for short periods — a few seconds)

DISCIPLINE STEP BY STEP

The primary activity of this era is to help your child link what he is feeling with what he is doing. Addressing his needs in that same sequence is extremely effective.

Below are two tried-and-true ways to cope with a discipline situation.

★ If the behavior has been aggressive or potentially dangerous and destructive:

Remove the child after one firm but calm warning, and take her to sit with you on a chair where you won't be interrupted. Face her toward you and remind her which family rule she has just broken (assuming you have discussed a few simple ones about the way you treat each other, etc.). Make eye contact, then listen to what she has to say, if anything. When both of you are sufficiently calm, return to the world and let it go.

If she continues to break the same rule, involve her in the solution. Ask what would help her to control her behavior in the future.

★ If your child is simply exhausted beyond functioning, and no felony has been committed:

Pick him up and take him to sit with you where you won't be interrupted. Describe what you think he might be feeling and what you are going to do to help: "It sure seems like you've had it, little guy. I think you need some quiet time with your dad, and when you are feeling better, we'll go back to be with everybody."

Mothers want their children to behave because it is good for kids to be good, and because it is easier for them to feel closer to their children and vice versa. The cultural expectation that mothers will teach their children to understand intimacy and relationships is served well by this "why" of behavior.

Fathers want their children to behave because it is good for kids to be good, and because it will be easier for them to find their way in the world if they behave more acceptably. A mother will sometimes imply, "Behave well for me because it hurts my feelings and our relationship when you don't." A father will sometimes imply, "Behave well because if you don't, you'll never get a job, have any friends, or get anywhere."

Of course, these are gross sexist and cultural stereotypes, but they show up in research over and over again — as trends only, not absolutes. Still these differing expectations play a role in the decisions that parents make about how to set limits for their children. Furthermore, kids exposed to both styles seem to show up later in life with better coping and problem-solving skills in both the social and academic domains.

Taming the Tantrums

One of the truly gnarly limit-pushers of this era is the temper tantrum. These are the hallmark of the self-control wars in the early years. They are distinct from the gut-wringing cries of the sick, wet, desperately hungry, or physically hurt infant or pretoddler. But they can look similar, and you can feel even more helpless.

Tantrums start to occur in that period of development when the "me do" surge for autonomy becomes increasingly frustrated by the parent who knows the toddler's abilities are still so limited that trouble lurks behind most corners. So when the child's limited ability frustrates a particular goal, or a parent intervenes to rein her in, the internal frustrations can erupt into a screaming, kicking, crying rage.

Every time you help your child recover from such a debacle without humiliation or irrational punishment, she learns that her impulses cannot destroy her world and that you can help her learn how to manage this tiger, the way you did the other tigers of her early years — being left alone, being helplessly hungry, etc.

Finally, two pieces of advice about limit setting and self-control that are hard for many parents to remember. When setting limits :

★ **The fewer words the better**

★ **Actions speak louder than words**

Fewer Words: My own decades of experience in clinical practice shows me that when parents use discipline phrases of more than 20 words, their children do not respond most of the time. If the emotional tone of that discipline

TACTICS FOR TANTRUMS

Know the choices *and transitions that are potential trouble spots in the autonomy travels:*

★ As he is playing with blocks and puzzles before lunch, give him a 10-minute and a five-minute warning. We all hate surprises when we are doing what we want.

★ Let him choose between his sweater and sweatshirt when dressing. No more, no less. Making simple choices helps a child feel in some control — self-control.

Once started, it's best for you to absent yourself from the tantrum scene, assuming the child is safe:

★ Getting you entangled usually escalates the trouble, particularly if you become upset and agitated, which of course you will the first few times, until you learn to stay calm and figure out what to do. Your absence helps the child use his own self-regulating mechanisms, the ones newly developed by the brain's learning from all the times you kept him safe and calm. (Discipline!)

★ The exception to leaving the scene of a tantrum is when the child is on center stage in a public place (typically the supermarket) and you feel the fool. Here the technique is different because the setting is so different. All too soon he realizes he has a captive audience — you and the rest of the store or train or bus — and he presses his advantage for all its worth. First, you must realize there is really no way to win here because your child, unlike you, couldn't care less what the hundreds of other people in the audience think of him or his behavior. The one thing you can do is remain calm. Then you can try explaining that he can't have what he wants here (no long explanation as to why it is inappropriate in this circumstance), but he can when he gets home. Then try distraction. If that fails, take him to the bathroom where the audience is smaller. If you still have no success, calmly and quietly leave the store. Ring down the curtain and kill the lights as quickly as you can. It is your only hope.

If, however, it's a big tantrum, one lasting for more than 5 minutes, then you will probably need to hold or hug him to help him settle physically before he can settle emotionally.

★ Simple chat: "You're so mad it's hard to talk. We'll calm down first."

Tantrums are generally not your fault, so don't act guilty and conciliatory.

★ That confuses your child, and short circuits the opportunity to manage these feelings, which are hers to learn to manage, with your help.

★ Nice-ing it out misses the opportunity to teach that internal control is the only way for your child to feel safe in the face of disappointment.

Don't reward tantrums.

is negative and nagging, the kids are practically deaf. This is so hard for many parents because we feel we are so right (actually righteous), compared to our kids. We want to believe that the more we correct them, the better they will behave. The data show exactly the opposite. These are some of my favorite ways to induce temporary preschool deafness:

- ★ **"Are you listening to me?" (What do YOU think?)**
- ★ **"How many times do I have to tell you?" (Apparently a lot)**
- ★ **"When I was little…" (You were perfect and that makes me the fool, right?)**
- ★ **"You never…always…will never…!" (A prophecy if I've ever heard one)**

I've always (oops), frequently, observed with my own children and countless others that, during brief periods of parental illness or absence, even young children will show leaps in mastery of personal-care habits and self-control. A powerful reminder of our limitations, and that self-control matters so much more than parent control.

Effective actions: Few words only works in the self-control area if you back it up with action. Otherwise, internal shame will turn into the humiliation of being useless. When your child bites someone during a visit, take him home after a simple reprimand, and don't endlessly berate him in his car seat. The action of losing his playtime speaks louder than anything you might say. Tossing a paper towel to a softly reprimanded child who has spilled juice while fooling around is a good one-two solution. Handing a spoon to a child who is provocatively mashing food into her mouth at dinner beats a lecture on manners.

One reason this two-part advice is so relevant during this period is that the child of 18 to 36 months has developed the ability to understand that you have feelings, too. This discovery makes your love and opinion of her matter deeply when she is struggling to develop more self-control. Showing her that her behavior affects the way you feel works in this era in a way that it hasn't before. Empathy and compassion begin to grow. When a child sees that her evolving self-control can make a parent feel good, too, the affirmation adds social and cognitive accomplishment to the achievement of controlling one's behavior.

Moral Behavior and Empathy

As with other aspects of behavior, moral behavior must be taught. One element of such behavior is the ability to empathize with others, to put oneself in someone else's shoes. Obviously, empathy can help inhibit anti-social behavior.

There is some evidence that empathy is part of a child's in-born temperament, and that some children are naturally more empathic than others. However, research also shows that empathic parents tend to have empathic children. So this important attribute is clearly shaped by example and teaching as well as by genes.

The ability to show children what it is to care about another's well being — physical and emotional — is central to teaching morality. It is also central to their self-control and their long-term ability to form lasting relationships.

Many childhood games are valuable for teaching connectedness, turn-taking and awareness of others. Peekaboo is a great example.

Summing Up

We have covered a lot of territory in this chapter. We've discussed a few specific crimes and misdemeanors and how to handle them. We've also discussed tantrums, nagging, and self-control. What does all this material tell us about the best ways to teach (note the replacement of the word *discipline*) self-control? This maxim sums it up well:

Learning self-control is the only way to achieve discipline

...in yourself and your child

...between yourself and your child

...that lasts long after they are past toddlerhood

...and punishment is hardly on the radar screen

We've learned that, during this 18- to 36-month period, the brain is primed to grow in the direction of more internal control if we feed it the right experiences as nutrients. During this period of development, children are developing a mind of their own, literally and figuratively. A child's healthy desire to explore, explain, and exploit bring her smack up against the world that must keep her safe, healthy, and in control.

Your main job, like it or not, is to convince your toddler that it is in her long-term best interest to learn to control her behavior. *Her* best interest, *not yours.* Of course, it makes your life easier when she behaves, but that is not the point. The point is for her to learn her own ways, to feel her own drives and impulses, but still settle down, feel safe, get angry, get loved, and take risks without putting herself in real danger, physically or emotionally. And she can't get there without help from you. But you must start, like solid foods, with small portions.

A Final Word

The last word in this chapter will be consistency. From the *Mishnah,* book of *Sukkah:*

Never promise something to a child and not give it to him, because in that way he learns to lie.

Consistency is key to success in the arena of limits. Without a good measure of it, a child can only be confused. Think through your priorities concerning your child's behavior. Occasionally revisit them. Adapt to your child's growth. And keep your focus on the long-term goals of your efforts: Self-control in your child; his good behavior and pleasing personality; a rewarding and enjoyable family life. Big ticket items that are well worth your investment. ★

CHAPTER 9

The World Beyond
Mom and Dad

The power, effect, and variety of experience with other
caretaking adults in and out of the home. The capacity to be alone.

In this chapter we explore what new research tells us about care at the hands of people other than our moms and dads. In our society, the vast majority of parents of young children work outside the home. As a result, we are intensely interested in how this works out for our children. Unfortunately, we are disturbingly passive as a country in our lack of support for quality care for all kids who need childcare outside their families. Preparing your child for it, preparing *yourself* for it, choosing a good spot (if you are lucky enough to have a choice), and what it means to your child will be the topics we focus on in this chapter.

As big a step as childcare, preschool, or any non-mom or -dad care is for the child, it's a bigger step for parents. It takes a lot of reassurance to settle the gnawing uncertainty about whether a child will be okay in the care of someone else.

The Understanding Child

Sadie loved her preschool. At 34 months, she was one of the older kids in her "2/3" group, and settled pretty comfortably after a month of attending three mornings each week. Her mother, however, was less certain that she was happy and felt the need to hang around after the other moms and dads left to make certain her daughter was okay. Sadie's new play buddy, Becca, was a few months younger, very chatty, and an avid partner in the dress-up corner. One morning, Becca, very aware of her friend's mother's presence, asked Sadie if her mother wanted to play dress-up with them. Sadie, as she picked through the morning's hat selection said quietly to her friend, "No, she just misses me and isn't ready to go."

An Issue of Trust

The success or failure of non-parental childcare hinges on the quality of all aspects of the process and the trust that flows from that quality:

Children: The transition to a new environment with one or more new caregivers (and probably other children) is a big one for toddlers. They need to learn from scratch that parents do come back, that other adults can be loving and trustworthy, and that other children can be fun to know and play with.

Parents: The transition to alternative care for their children is just as big for parents. They need to be comfortable with their choice to use alternative care, and they need to have confidence in the alternative they choose.

The benefits of alternative care for children and parents depend on the quality of care parents invest in and how well parents, themselves, manage the routine for their children. Sadly, research shows many gaps between the ideal and reality.

For starters, polls show parents have a hard time trusting the people they choose to care for their kids. Sixty percent of all children three years old and younger are in non-parental care. But in a 1997 poll by Zero to Three: National Center for Infants, Toddlers and Families, *only 2% of parents mentioned their child's caregiver as someone they usually turn to for help on parenting issues.* So much for parental comfort with their choice.

Moreover, parents often operate on wrong assumptions about what's really best for their child. For example, 58% of parents in the Zero to Three poll believed that the more caregivers a child has before age three, the better the child will adapt to change. Not true.

Infants and toddlers do better with *fewer* caregivers — a small number with whom the children can build the trust that makes it *worth* behaving for someone they love. If there are too many caregivers, children can be overwhelmed by so many caretaker styles. They end up not building trust for other adults, and their day is marked more by uncertainty than by warmth and consistency. This is one reason parents should look for childcare options that provide a lot of one-on-one interaction between child and caregiver as well as low turnover among caregivers.

There are a number of alternatives for non-parental childcare:

★ **Extended family members care for your child at their place or yours.**

★ **A sitter comes to your home.**

★ **A nanny or au pair cares for your child in your home.**

★ **One or two adults look after a small group of children, often of mixed ages, in a home-based situation.**

★ **A staff looks after small groups of children divided into various age groups at a commercial childcare center.**

★ **Children are cared for in a commercial-style center where you work.**

Preschool for two- to four-year-olds offers another option that mixes care with a beginning emphasis on instruction. For a child to be ready for preschool, he must have moved beyond the emotional dependency of toddlerhood and progressed to the "instrumental dependency" of the preschool years. At this stage, children seek help with tasks that are beyond their abilities, and they look to adults for praise and to share discoveries. However, they are able to follow a few simple rules and regulate their emotions without constant guidance from an adult. They know that certain acts produce predictable consequences.

These developments in the preschooler lay the foundation for relationships with other children. Growing emotional maturity and independence allow children to relate emotionally to one another (essential to having a good time), to understand the basics of play (such as give-and-take), and to manage to some degree the inevitable tensions that arise (when both children want the same toy *now*).

Whatever choice you make, it is a highly personal decision and should be made after lots of thought and talk with people who know kids and your child in particular. In this chapter, we will look at criteria for telling the good from the bad, since those criteria stay roughly the same from one childcare setting to another.

Childcare: Helpful or Harmful?

The most important study ever undertaken on the effects of early childcare was begun in 1991 by the National Institute of Child Health and Human Development. This long-term research project enrolled 1,364 families from diverse circumstances in 10 locales around the country when their babies were one month old. The families themselves chose the form of childcare, which included care by fathers, care by other relatives, in-home caregivers, childcare home providers, and center-based care.

Throughout the project, researchers have collected information about the children's development according to the type, amount, and quality of care provided. Early reports have provided sobering findings as data has been analyzed, though the scientific community advises that it is still too early to call *all* the findings significant. Nonetheless, good quality childcare is shown to provide some small but measurable benefits. When childcare is not at its best, however, children do less well.

According to the data, *better results* relate only to children in *higher quality childcare.* As the report states:

"The **quality** of childcare during the first three years of life is consistently but modestly associated with children's cognitive and language development. The higher the quality of childcare (more positive language stimulation and interaction between the child and provider), the greater the child's language abilities at 15, 24, and 36 months, the better the child's cognitive development at age two and the more school readiness the child showed at age three."[1]

---

[1] *The NICHD Study of Early Childcare*, National Institute of Child Health and Human Development, April, 1998.

SUMMARY OF NICHD FINDINGS ON CHILDCARE[2]

Higher Quality Care was Related to:	Lower Quality Care Predicted:
Better mother-child relationships	Less harmonious mother-child relationships
Lower probability of insecure attachment in infants of mothers low in sensitivity	A higher probability of insecure mother-child attachment of mothers who are already low in sensitivity to their children
Fewer reports of children's problem behaviors	More problem behaviors
Higher cognitive performance of children in childcare	Lower cognitive ability
Higher children's language ability	Lower language ability
Higher level of school readiness	Lower school readiness scores

In looking at childcare characteristics, such as quality, age of entry into care, type, and stability:

"Researchers determined that childcare characteristics were, at best, modest predictors of children's problem behavior, compliance and self-control. Childcare quality was the most consistent predictor of children's behavior. Children in care receiving more sensitive and responsive attention had fewer caregiver-reported problems at age two and three."[3]

These early findings are informative and we cannot ignore their implications. As shown in the summary chart above, on the study's findings, childcare that is mediocre or worse takes a toll on children and on the important relationships in their lives outside of childcare.

[2] Ibid.
[3] Ibid.

How Much Childcare Is Too Much?

A real battleground exists around the issue of "How much childcare is too much childcare?" The research struggles to shed more light than heat on this matter. A major contributor in the area, Jay Belsky from Pennsylvania State University, conducted a study in 1996 that concluded that when children experienced 20 or more hours per week of non-maternal care during the first year, there were greater risks of family troubles during the second year.

"Family troubles" meant more coercive parent-toddler interchanges and less family satisfaction or pride regarding the toddler's autonomy and independence. The issue of quality when discussing "non-maternal care" is highly problematic. And as we have already seen, trouble in childcare is a risk factor itself, probably independent of the time involved.

Other research by Megan Gunner of the University of Minnesota is intriguing and worrisome. She measures levels of cortisol, a "stress hormone," in the saliva of children in potentially stressful situations. She feels that this shows how a child responds biologically to a particular care setting. In chaotic, non-nurturing childcare settings with high staff turnover, insufficient individual attention to kids, and little parental involvement, even the youngest children show signs of physiological and biochemical distress through high levels of cortisol in their saliva. Such high levels can interfere with a child's ability to focus, retain instruction, or regulate emotions.

Alan Schore weighs in on the matter of stress in poor quality childcare as well, explaining that emotional interactions that are confusing, unsatisfying, and unresolved (as is so often the case in poor quality care settings) actually alter the brain in ways that have long-term effects on mood-regulating systems. That, in turn, changes the child's motivational functions. If kids can't get heard or understood, eventually they give up, and they lose their motivation.

A Missed Opportunity

Trish, 32 months old, was one of 21 toddlers and young preschoolers in a child-care center housed in a strip mall for the convenience of parents who worked in the suburban sprawl nearby. It was clean, well-lighted, and friendly, but was chronically understaffed. One morning Trish was in the book corner reading when she suddenly recognized a letter as being in her name. Thrilled, she jumped to her feet, folded the book under her arm and crossed the room to her favorite teacher, who was preoccupied mediating a dispute in the block corner that had turned violent. She waited as long as she could, and then turned to another teacher. Unfortunately, her second choice was preparing the morning snack and told Trish she'd have to wait. Trish then went to the half-time aide who told her she "wasn't doing reading this morning yet." Twelve minutes was just too long for Trish. She went back to the book corner and said, "I hate books," and dejectedly threw the book down as though *it* were the problem. Apparently it was.

Ronald Lally of Far West Laboratory in San Francisco notes that, despite the growth of the number of children under one year old now in childcare situations, little attention has been paid to the long-term impact of non-parental care on the formation of the child's identity. He points out that most infant and toddler childcare programs were developed by people whose experience was working with older children, not little ones. He also notes that too many people underestimate the importance of care in these early years. This is changing as parents learn more about infant development. But we have a long way to go.

Dr. Lally recommends limiting the number of caregivers for a child and that caregivers be of the same culture and speak the same language as the child's family. He also recommends that children be cared for in small groups, that they have ample opportunity to learn and discover on their own terms, and that caregivers be highly responsive to individual needs and preferences.

These recommendations may sound simple and common sense. Unfortunately, they are not the norm. As you have seen throughout this book, the power of a caregiver to influence a child's development is great. Yet, childcare workers are so woefully underpaid, it is hard for them to feel valued enough to be emotionally present in the ways that good care demands. And many factors, including conditions at the childcare facility, can affect the relationship between child and caregiver — for good or ill.

Substandard Childcare — Exception or the Rule?

The University of Colorado and the Families and Work Institute in New York City joined with the NICHD in reporting that 60% to 80% of available daycare is inadequate for very young children. Dr. Edward Ziegler, friend and colleague at Yale as well as founder of Head Start in the late 1960s, has summarized his landmark meta-analysis of the quality of childcare in America with this sobering breakdown: 20% are good, 40% are minimally acceptable, and 40% are harmful. Chilling news.

Kids need ongoing, long-term, loving relationships, enriched by language and sensory stimulation, lively emotional engagement, and many learning opportunities in order to become whole. Most of us in the field of child development feel that, during the first 24 to 30 months, the majority of the child's waking life needs to be spent interacting like this through the magic and power of everyday moments. The benefits of this kind of interaction can't be achieved in sporadic bursts of "quality time." *It is the quality of quantity time that shapes the adult your child will become.*

Sadly, this level of care in long-lasting relationships is too rarely available at childcare centers. Only gas station attendants have shorter job longevity than childcare workers.

Signs of High-Quality Childcare

Now that we have thought about the importance of good care for kids, let's think about how to judge a given setting. This is no time to be shy or overaccommodating. Sometimes, in the desire not to offend, we demand more of our animal sitters than we do of our childsitters. Don't be afraid to ask lots of questions, snoop around, and check everything out. Even if your beloved aunt has offered to help, let her know, as you would anyone, what your expectations are, and ask every question you can think of. If she balks, think again. What is more precious to you, her feelings or your child's well-being?

The Importance of the Caregiver

Of all the important aspects of childcare, none is more important than the relationship between your child and the caregiver. Whether you are choosing a center or seeking someone to work in your home, the caregiver's training, patience, warmth, and enjoyment of your child is critical to your child's well-being.

You should look for someone who is warm, loving, and responsive, and who can pay close attention to your child and respond to his individual needs, praising his achievements and supporting his development. This kind of relationship teaches a child that other adults can be trustworthy and enjoyable. It also provides the level and variety of stimulation that is essential for healthy brain growth and optimal development on all fronts during this critical 18- to 36-month period.

At this age, your child still depends heavily on adults for stimulation. She is not yet able to amuse or teach herself for long periods of time. If her caregiver doesn't pay enough attention, your child's development will suffer.

A good caregiver, on the other hand, can be a wonderful resource for parents — an excellent source of information and helpful observations of their child's progress. It pays to get to know your child's caregiver, to brief her in the morning about anything eventful, to get an update from her at the end of each day, and to arrange periodic meetings for you and your spouse or partner to discuss your child.

WHAT TO LOOK FOR IN CHILDCARE

The Basics

★ Be sure your center is licensed by the state. Also, check with the state department that regulates childcare to see if any complaints have been filed against this particular setting and, if so, what they were.

★ Look for centers where there is one caregiver for every five children from 18 to 24 months of age, and one caregiver for every six children from 24 to 36 months of age.

★ Is there someone present who is licensed in CPR?

★ Are the phones regularly answered at the setting by *people*?

★ Are references readily available?

Inspection

★ Is the space cheerful, bright, and inviting?

★ Does it have clean, well-lighted, safe spaces?

★ Does it look and smell like a fun place to be?

★ Is the noise level acceptable?

★ Do you see many children crying?

★ Are there well-organized toy and pretend/play areas?

★ Are there quiet areas for rest and sleep?

★ Does the center have a program to build strong, balanced growth in emotional, social, cognitive and physical skills?

★ Is each child encouraged to be curious and creative?

★ Does the center provide daily reports to parents about the child's activities?

★ Is the center flexible enough to meet your family's needs?

★ Are the educational and art materials age-appropriate, and are the books and musical instruments attractive, easily accessible, and in good repair?

★ Check out the kitchen, bathrooms and outside play areas for safety and access. Especially check out the safeguards to prevent children from wandering off.

★ Check out the written policies regarding illness, closings, and pick ups. Make sure the center has secure procedures regarding pick ups by people other than parents.

★ Does the center welcome unannounced visits? Such visits are an excellent quality control. If they aren't allowed, your red flag should go up.

Watching

Pay close attention to the quality of attention children receive. Also look to see how well the center's written policies and procedures are followed.

★ Are the caregivers well-trained, warm, friendly and energetic?

★ Are there enough caregivers so that your child will get individual attention? Again, there should be one caregiver for every five children from 18 to 24 months of age, and one caregiver for every six children from 24 to 36 months of age.

★ How do the caregivers respond to children? Quickly? Sensitively?

★ Do care providers wash their hands before and after food or bodily-care activities?

★ See how the caregivers manage the comings and goings of parents and children.

★ Are parents encouraged to linger to allow the child to settle in each day?

★ Do members of the staff and the children seem to enjoy one another?

★ Do staff members make good eye contact with the kids and relate to them in ways that show they understand each child's temperament and style?

★ Watch the application of policies regarding pickup by folks unknown to the center.

Trial Period

★ Give yourself three weeks to see if this thing is going to work for you and your child.

★ See how caregivers or supervisors handle your needs regarding cancellations, illness, medications, etc.

★ Make an unannounced visit, *especially* if such visits are discouraged. What's the center like when you have given no warning of your visit? How does the center handle you? Defensiveness on their part is not a good sign.

★ See how much variety your child has in daily activities. Children need variety and new experiences to grow.

Worrisome Signs

These should raise your eyebrows and get your attention because they could mean your center falls in that unfortunate 60 to 80% that are inadequate, and your child is unlikely to benefit from hanging around this particular spot.

★ There is a high rate of staff turnover (average stays are in months, not years).

★Other parents complain frequently.

★Accidents occur without plausible explanations.

★There is resistence to parental involvement (mothers and fathers) in programming.

★There is chronic refusal to address your worries.

★Caregivers resist discussing your child's complaints and/or persistent unhappiness.

★Your child resists, or persistently complains about, a caregiver or child in the group, or suddenly refuses to go to childcare, especially after initial acceptance.

★Your child shows growing disinterest in learning and discovery.

★Your child is increasingly withdrawn, or you notice sudden changes in behavior or expression of negative emotions that don't seem attributable to anything happening at home.

★More time is spent discussing fees and schedules than philosophy and policies.

Signs of High Quality

★Strong encouragement of parental involvement.

★Exceptionally warm, patient and attentive staff that stay for years.

★Caregivers who have training in early childhood education and practice age-appropriate activities.

★Discipline that is grounded in talking through and re-direction, not punishment and shame. Shame is so powerful as an interactive tool with young children that it is best left at home where it is part of loving and trusting relationships.

A Sad Irony

Edward Ziegler points out an interesting irony regarding quality childcare in America. He describes a "three-tiered system" of childcare in the U.S. The well- and very well-to-do get the best care because they demand and pay for it. The next best tier goes to the poor and very poor because the government is funding and monitoring it. The largest and worst tier of care is the one available to average-income families.

It is a deplorable Catch-22: Those families in which both parents work to keep the family above the poverty level cannot, therefore, receive the quality childcare they could get if their income were below the poverty level. As a result, *the majority of the nation's children who receive childcare are in the poorest facilities.*

Equally sad is that when a family somehow knows this and feels it has no alternative, that family may choose not to see what is happening. After they have made their childcare choice, some parents don't check out the quality of care. One grandmother told me that her daughter and son-in-law had never been to the childcare center except to pick up and drop off the child because, "If they actually had to see it was that bad, they would only feel worse. What could they do? It is their only choice."

Preparing for the Move to Childcare

So you've done your homework, checked out the childcare options, and selected the people or center to care for your child. Now you are approaching the first day when you will leave your little one in the care of someone else on a regular basis.

This is wrenching for every parent. In fact, most babies and young children adapt to their new environment more easily than parents do. And it's important for parents to appreciate and care for their own emotions at this juncture.

Preparing Your Child for the Transition to Childcare

As with so many things for young children, taking it slow and easy can work wonders. If your child is moving into alternative childcare for the first time during this 18- to 36-month period, make the transition gradual, providing lots of support.

MANAGING PARENTAL EMOTIONS

★*Don't pretend you're fine, just fine, when you're not.* It's much better to acknowledge your feelings. It's normal to feel grief at this change. You will come through sooner and better if you face your feelings head on.

★*Don't believe you are a bad parent for choosing childcare.* If you have chosen a good center or caregiver, you can be confident that your child is in good hands, so there is no logical reason to feel guilty. But if you continue to feel guilty, it's important to come to grips with these feelings. Be especially alert if you are tempted to change your parenting style. For example, some parents start easing up on setting limits to compensate for their guilt. Such behavior leads nowhere you or your child want to go.

★*Don't become critical of your child's caregiver.* It's important to have a good relationship with caregivers. Their observations and advice can be extremely helpful to your parenting. If you find you feel critical even though the caregiver's work doesn't merit such an attitude, recognize that your feelings are a part of the separation process. Then begin to focus on the caregiver's talents and good qualities. Rest assured that no caregiver will take your place in your child's life or heart. The new attachments to other warm and loving caregivers are beneficial. They also are good signs of your child's emotional maturity and your achievement in nurturing that maturity.

★*Don't understate the importance of the transition to childcare.* If you pretend the new routine doesn't matter, you may underestimate the good things that can come from this new experience for your child and you — new friends, new learning, new sources of information, and new ideas on parenting.

★**Make sure your child meets the caregivers or teachers before moving into this new environment. If you choose a childcare center or preschool, make sure your child knows at least one other child in the class. If your child doesn't already know someone, ask the caregiver to suggest one or two children who might be good matches for your child, and set up a few play dates.**

★ Talk to your child about the new arrangement, describing the friends to be made and the wonderful things to be done and learned. Talk about being apart and getting back together. Play games such as hide-and-seek that demonstrate being apart and together.

★ When moving to a new childcare arrangement, start gradually, if possible. For example, allow your child to be alone with a new nanny or at a new childcare center for short periods at first, and then slowly increase the time away from you.

★ Once the new arrangements are underway, get up a bit earlier so you have time together before you leave. Also, make special family times in the evenings and on weekends.

★ Let your child take her favorite toy or "softie" to school.

★ Tell the caregiver or teacher of any factors that might influence your child's behavior or needs for the day, such as a restless night, family illness, or visits from relatives.

★ Be aware that separation anxiety may come and go in cycles. You can ease your child's upsets if you make your departure warm and smooth, staying long enough to let your child settle in, but without lingering. And *never* sneak out or lie, telling your little one you "will be right back" just before you dash to the parking lot. Your child needs to be able to rely on his trust in you as he navigates this new world.

★ When you pick your child up, ask the caregiver about what happened during the day. Then discuss the day's events with your child.

Some children have occasional meltdowns at the end of the day when parents arrive to pick them up. While this can be heart-wrenching for parents, it's a normal release of the child's emotions built up during the day. Children away from home tend to take their involvement down a notch or two, napping less deeply and playing less intensely than when they are at home. The welcome sight of mom or dad uncorks the backlog. Extra hugs and reassurances will help set the stage for peace and calm in the evening. These meltdowns will decrease in time. Just keep reassuring your child and maintain consistency in your routines.

Meltdowns can be made worse by an abrupt pick up. A child engrossed in a project when a parent arrives may not welcome being yanked away. Try to arrive a little early at pick up time to allow your child to finish up and make a smoother transition to going home.

The Significance of Child's Play

A central development of this 18- to 36-month period is a child's evolving ability to play with other children and to build friendships. The traditional pattern for this evolution starts before age two with what is called "imitative play," in which one or more children copy the actions of another. Children also play independently side-by-side in what is called "parallel play." The next step, generally by age three, is genuine interaction, albeit not entirely harmonious. There can be bickering over who plays with what toy, and sharing does not come naturally at first. (Parental teaching-by-example is invaluable here.)

THE NEED TO FEEL SECURE

The need to feel secure is a serious matter when children are out of their parents' care. Their emotional cues are the key to understanding what can help them in being comfortable and appropriately dependent. From thumb-sucking and pacifiers to "loveys and softies," children must be allowed to discover and use the props that help them to comfort themselves and manage stress, especially when parents are absent. That children can use these props and tactics is a testament to their parents' success in helping them to cope with life's discomforts and uncertainties.

These objects are transitional. As children grow in their capacities to adapt to and manage change and troublesome emotions, they usually will give them up on their own. I advise parents not to take them away, especially during these transitions. On the contrary. Keep them in good repair! I have seen blankets and toys that were rags and shadows of their former selves, glued, patched, and restitched, still providing soothing magic.

Thumb-sucking into the second year can cause some tooth disruption if it is especially intense and prolonged. Pacifiers are kinder to the mouth and teeth because they distribute sucking pressure more evenly throughout the mouth. By the first birthday, the need for non-nutritive sucking usually starts to diminish, so that by 18 months, walking and talking are picking up the self-stimulation slack. Comforting should be spread out over rocking, cuddling, softies, etc., lessening the appetite for sucking.

However, the path and speed of this evolutionary process is not set in stone and, in fact, is easily altered by group childcare. In group settings, children under two can and do play together, and learn turn-taking, sharing, and an element of cooperation. These come about as cognitive development grows and leads children to understand order and sequence. For example, a child may push a nearby object toward another child who is reaching for it. Researchers say this reflects a natural desire for completion of a natural sequence of expected events, rather than empathy or an emotional response to the desire or need of the other child. Yet this desire for completion lays the foundation for later empathy and emotion-based social behavior.

Early Friends

Sam, age 25 months, sat contentedly in the middle of the den surrounded by the contents of a spilled bucket of plastic fruit. As he hummed distractedly, he busily matched the fruit according to his own internal sense of classification – sometimes size, sometimes color, sometimes texture. His cousin Alice, 21 months old, sat about six feet away, systematically tearing up *The New York Times Sunday Magazine* slowly and deliberately, half page by half page. The sound seemed as interesting to her as the tactile sensation of tearing, not to mention the sheer joy in the act of destruction. When she completed her task and sat back to survey the glorious mess, Sam then pushed the *TV Guide* to within her grasp without saying anything, as if he knew she was hungry for more. He returned to his sorting without a single social reference to his cousin's play, as Alice set to work again.

Preschools

Preschool is a particular form of childcare with a commitment to skill building and school readiness down the road. An estimated five million children are in preschool programs, and the number is growing. According to studies done by the Families and Work Institute of New York, children benefit from good programs with competent staff and good ratios. They suffer fewer behavioral troubles, have larger expressive vocabularies, feel close to their teachers, and enjoy more complex, less aggressive play with peers.

Children become ready for preschool at different times. A two-year-old who enjoys regular play dates with peers is probably ready to try some group learning experiences in exercise or music once or twice a week. A few hours of preschool per day might then be the next step, beginning two to three days a week and moving toward five days.

Typical requisite preschool skills for two-year-olds:

★ Is actively working on separating from you when you drop her off.

★ Practices self-care skills, like hand-washing.

★ Is learning to share instead of being possessive.

★ Uses expressive, not just receptive speech.

Preschools can help a great deal here by having children listen to both read and told stories, and then discussing their content. This encourages a sense of cooperation by listening and playing with others, and rehearsing self-reliance by helping with group chores.

Typical requisite preschool skills for three-year-olds:

★ Is learning how to play cooperatively with others.

★ Is learning to express powerful feelings.

★ Can feel pride in his own accomplishments.

★ Feels increasingly okay at greater distances from you, and…

★ Tries to be less impulsive by thinking before he acts.

The preschool can assist by helping him practice his sharing skills in the play times of his day, directing him to learn more language through imaginative play, songs and stories, and inhibit his aggressive impulses and to "use his words, not his hands" to problem solve.

Some preschools are expanding to offer childcare to infants who then move into the preschool curriculum as they grow.

A Time for Change

Lest we become too discouraged about finding good quality care, remember there is much we can do to change the way our population thinks about the needs of our youngest children when not in the full-time care of their parents. Many dedicated professionals are working hard to educate parents and public officials about the importance of quality care in early childhood. Some ideas:

★ Child development and family life courses need to be taught with the regularity and fervor of drug prevention programs in our middle schools. The need is so great that it should become part of the curriculum and extend over several years.

★ Consistency in staffing at childcare centers needs to be supported to reduce turnover and improve quality. Efforts to organize childcare workers by AFL-CIO have recently begun and, though controversial, have helped to raise public awareness that the standards for reimbursement and employment conditions are unacceptably low in the childcare industry. Conditions must improve so that the dedicated and trained caregivers do not burn-out or leave because they cannot make a decent wage or achieve the level of professional recognition they merit.

★ Unfortunately, the arithmetic of caregiver compensation doesn't offer much hope. In the guidelines given earlier, one caregiver should be responsible for no more than six children aged 24 to 36 months — a big load as any parent of a toddler knows. Yet this means that the tuition from only six families must pay for the facility, management, supplies, and all other overhead, *plus* the caregiver's salary and beneifts. No wonder high-quality care is found mostly in expensive settings and in those that are subsidized by government or religious institutions.

★ Edward Ziegler's "Schools for the 21st Century" project suggests that the existing infrastructure of school and community schools include quality childcare and health care. His idea is that communities already recognize schools as centers of effort on behalf of children, at least in principle. They need to use their buildings to provide health and other support services (including childcare) for the children attending the existing school, instead of requiring families to accommodate to the needs of a whole other institution of care, such as a hospital clinic, or corporate childcare that is physically and often ideologically and culturally separated from the community.

None of this is easy but the hypocrisy has got to stop, and soon.

Once again Oribasius sets the standard of care for curriculum selection appropriately high 1600 years ago:

As for teachers:

It is not necessary to torment children just beginning to learn by trying to teach them something through the whole length of the day: on the contrary the greater part of the day should be devoted to their games. ★

CHAPTER 10

Boys and Girls Together

Using what we know in everyday life.

As the ultrasound technician skillfully glided the probe over my wife's four-month pregnant and oiled abdomen, she lay (and I stood) in awestruck silence as we "met" our TV baby for the first time. Face (her mom's profile!), hands, backbone, femur, a random foot — all danced in and out of the snowy video plains flying across the monitor.

Having seen hundreds of fetal ultrasounds, I knew what to look for as she neared the lower abdomen…A girl! The technician and I recognized the echo of the vaginal labia, but said nothing. However, Marsha sensed the change in our attention. We agreed that we wanted to know the sex if it was discernible, but I trusted the technician's skill more than mine. Marsha and I looked at each other, agreed to ask, and the tech confirmed: "She's all girl!"

Like many slightly older parents, we felt a whisper of a lean toward having a girl, and felt pleasure at the news. But as the day wore on, I became more uncertain about what having this knowledge would mean for the next five months. As we talked, I discovered a slight disappointment that we knew the gender, and would have to wait so long to meet the rest of her, which, after all, was the really important part of being a girl, or a boy, for that matter. This seemed to lend a kind of artificial significance to gender as a trait. Maybe it was better to meet your baby's gender at the same time you meet the rest of her/him. In that way, gender is just one more wonderful thing that makes your baby special.

In general, gender probably constricts a child's world less than it does the child's parents' world, given cultural and societal norms. Still, the differences intrigue and confound us, and it is worth knowing how those differences shape the toddler and preschool years so that we can be appropriately supportive.

But first: a disclaimer supported so strongly by my own experience that I only reluctantly write this chapter:

Boys' and girls' developmental similarities greatly overshadow the differences.

Still, the toddler's discovery that all bodies are not similarly equipped introduces one of the first great mysteries of life. And to be honest, *vive la différence* never loses its seductive fascinations for any of us. Having that said, let's explore the differences that exist and what significance, if any, they have on the way that kids grow up in our care.

Differences Before and After Birth

There is an age-old debate about whether boys and girls are born with behavioral differences, or whether the differences are the result of parents treating boys and girls differently.

Researchers have found behavioral differences between genders that are evident even before birth — clearly before anyone has had an opportunity to influence behavior. For example, we now understand that sex hormones (estrogen and testosterone) shape the central nervous system in utero to predispose boys and girls to perceive their worlds slightly differently. Male fetuses are more active than females of similar birth weights.

We also see differences in types and levels of activity very early on. After birth, newborn boys move their limbs and torsos around more than girls. Meanwhile, baby girls show less overall action and movement, but when touched, show greater reactivity than boys. Within six months of birth, girls are slightly more reactive to human faces.

Researchers also have found physiological differences between genders that may account for behavioral differences. For example, neuroscientist Patricia Goldman-Rakic of Yale found a decade ago that male and female brains differed anatomically in ways that could explain the language and communication strengths common in girls and the *tendency* toward spatial and motoric strengths in boys. Since then, gonadal (sexual) hormones also have been implicated in shaping the differences in regulation of emotion and aggression in these same areas of the brain.

This becomes even more intriguing now that we have learned that these are the very areas of the central nervous system responsible for striking a balance between excitatory activity and inhibitory activity. Boys and girls may not follow the same path in using experience to shape the wiring of these mood-regulating centers of the brain, called the limbic system.

The Role of Nurture

Despite these findings, parenting practices play a huge role in shaping different behavior patterns for boys and girls.

For example, classic behavioral conditioning studies done 30 years ago showed that boys in newborn nurseries who were dressed in pink and girls in blue were treated very differently by adults of both genders. "Blue" (presumed male) babies were handled more robustly and talked to less, while "pink" (presumed female) babies were handled more gently and talked to more, and more sweetly at that. And that is only the beginning.

Parents tend to hold their male infants upright more often than girls (boys "seem" less cuddly), and they hold them more often. Is this because they are more restless and active and need the extra holding, or is it because mothers and fathers prefer little boys to be more active from the start? After six months, when infants begin to sit up, it is the girls that get held more, as boys are encouraged to belly around the environment and explore (training for the hunter?).

To further complicate the picture, developmentalists and pediatricians have noticed that the child of the opposite sex enjoys a particular appeal to each of their parents. This shows up in disciplinary styles. Parents tend to set limits with more authority and brook less guff with a child of the same gender. It's as though the parent feels and acts: "I know *exactly* what you are thinking — been there, done it, don't try it." The opposite gender parent of course, hasn't been *exactly* there, lacks the confidence, and feels a bit off balance as a result.

Gender Identity

Adding to the mix is the child's growing awareness of his or her own gender identity and what that means in the context of daily life. The period of greatest activity in the specialization of mood, behavior, and gender interconnections seems to be in the middle of the second year. The sensual exhibitionism that parents come to expect (dread? fear? enjoy?) in their 18- to 20-month-old toddler is the clue that the maturing brain has made the right connections between gender, body image, and emotional regulation. What parents need to know is that boys and girls will develop emotionally and cognitively in slightly different ways from this point forward. Let the games begin.

There appears to be a kind of "great divide" in gender identity that occurs somewhere around 20 to 24 months. Beyond this time, a child cannot reverse what he or she feels emotionally about being a boy or a girl. Neither can parents undo this meaning to him or her, making emotional sexual reassignment practically impossible after two years of being raised as a specific gender. Another example of the importance of the early wiring of the brain's architecture.

Out in the world, other trends are observable. By their first birthday, boys *tend* to be more diligent and less easily frustrated in visual-spatial tasks, such as stacking and building, shape sorting, etc. Their overall play tends to be more motor-dominated and physically aggressive than girls' play. Girls, meanwhile, lean toward more socially complex interactions that are less motor dominated, and they react more to subtle cues, such as soft words and smiles. (A reminder that these are generalities. We all know girls and boys with traits of the opposite gender.)

Once started, these trends seem to gather momentum, but not without help. Clearly, parents adjust quickly and powerfully to these early cues. In the end, parental responses and reinforcements probably outweigh these early predispositions in solidifying them into eventual bedrock difference.

So far, the physiological bases for different traits and behavior certainly exist, but they appear relatively broad and indeterminate. Despite the best efforts of parents and experts to reduce the power of sexual stereotyping in child rearing, this gender stuff dies hard indeed. Clearly our behavior toward our little boys and little girls shapes much of the outcome. Once again, it is how we nurture nature that matters most.

Vive la Difference!

There are many observations regarding male and female newborns and infants that convince us that there is more than just personality at work in giving our children their life-long traits. Still, classifications that uniformly differentiate male from female are less common. For this discussion we will try to shed more light than heat by laying out behavioral trends more characteristic of boys, and then do the same for girls. You undoubtedly know boys who sound like these girls and vice versa. Again, *vive la difference!* The point of this exercise is to help you appreciate who your toddler is becoming and what are the forces shaping him or her into a preschooler and beyond in the matter of gender.

Laying out these oversimplifications side by side helps us to see how these trends can lead us to treat very young children differently based on, or strongly influenced by, gender. According to the *American Journal of Preventive Medicine*, the high activity level of boys shows up in the disturbing statistic that boys age three and under are 23% more likely to show up at the emergency room or doctor's office for injury than are girls. This predisposition toward action gives boys' activity levels that "always causing a commotion" quality. Little female explorers are more likely to verbalize when they explore

TRENDS: BOYS VS. GIRLS

Trends in Boys Being Boys	Trends in Girls Being Girls
Boy babies are more physically active in the womb, parental bed, basinet, crib, bunk bed, etc. than girls.	Girl babies tend to be less active overall in the womb, parental bed, etc.
Gross motor activity is preferred over fine motor activity for most boys, leading them to explore as soon as they can crawl.	Girls generally prefer fine motor to gross motor activities as they get older. So even though they may have learned to crawl quite well, their radius of exploration is smaller than that of a male counterpart.
Boys tend to cause a ruckus when they want something, such as a possession or access to something forbidden.	Girls are more likely to misbehave and whine when they feel they need attention.
Boys tend to rely less on vocalization or verbal skills during social interaction than girls and can play for extended periods of time quite silently, except for crashing and banging about.	Girls tend to rely on verbal and vocalization as part of communication and generally speak conversationally earlier than boys.
Boys tend to be more impulsive, with less energy or interest devoted to internal controls or inhibition of negative behavior.	Girls are less impulsive in general and have greater inhibitory controls over behavior.
	Girl infants are more likely than boys to respond to the soft touch, soft voice and / or a smiling face.

out of eyesight of a parent, whereas parents of boys are more likely to be alerted by a worrisome thud in the next room, rather than a social squeal.

Again, Harvard's Jerome Kagan cautions us that girls are not just being "good" here, but may, in fact, be demonstrating their higher awareness of unfamiliar people and places than boys. What makes girls feel "good" is that such behavior is "lower maintenance" for very busy parents.

The implications for boys with their higher action appetite is that they more frequently run afoul of adults trying to keep order or to a schedule, be it at home or in groups of kids at a childcare center, preschool, or play group. It has been repeatedly shown that it is the *expectation* to "sit still and behave" that is more the problem, and less the boy's "distractability." Boys are three to four times more likely than girls to be diagnosed with attention, hyperactive, or learning problems later in school. And we find exponentially greater use of drugs to manage boys' behavior as opposed to girls' behavior.

As girls curry slightly more favor in group care from their largely female caregiving staffs, this does not mean that managing little girls is uniformly easier than managing little boys. As little boys work out their aggressive predispositions on the playground and in the block corner, little girls work out their aggression in the dress-up or doll corner. Three-year-old girls playing "mommy games" are frequently seen withholding affection, even bottles from troublesome and "fussy" or "bad" pretend babies who "don't listen to" their diminutive mommies. Even at home, they explore the social and relational power of withheld affection.

"I want a story"

Genny was mighty irritated at her mother for breast feeding her new little brother when she needed her to read to her "NOW, not later, NOW!" and "Daddy didn't read good stories." After it was clear that her mother wasn't budging, the 34-month-old princess turned on her heel and harrumphed as she crossed her arms stomping out of the room pronouncing, "I don't love you Mommy. I love my poohby (her Pooh bear) now!"

The Big Discovery

At the end of the first year, most kids have discovered the comfort and soothing pleasure that comes with "holding your own" (genitals, that is). It couldn't be more normal, and it has an important place in valuing one's own body. Parents, of course, have the job over the next year of socializing this bit of behavior. Instruction in privacy usually helps but shame does not.

Six months later, driven by innate curiosity about *other* people's pleasures and equipment, the child discovers that not all bodies are created the same. It's a rare 18-month-old that hasn't wormed her way into the bathroom of even the most demure parent to watch a mom or pop toilet or shower.

This new level of interest seems to begin with what looks like an unrelated event — the ability to walk. Developmentalists for 50 years have noted the relationship between becoming upright and increased interest in one's own genitals. Is it as simple as having one's hands free and conveniently hanging at just the right level to explore one's own genital equipment? Or is it that the central nervous and the genital-sensory systems have matured sufficiently between 12 and 18 months that genital self-stimulation becomes a favorite soother possible for boys and girls?

Whatever the reasons, once toddlers discover the sensory delights of holding and exploring their genitals, they put a lot of time and effort into the pursuit. As with everything else they have done to date, this proceeds without regard to its social consequence. Children are often bewildered when they are teased or shamed about this new discovery of which they are so proud.

Now the child tries to apply what she understands about the world to this incredible discovery. Little girls often struggle with the idea that a penis might be worth having since their own equipment seems less obvious or suitable for exhibition. Is it better (as with all possessions), given the choice to have a thing rather than not have it? She may spend some time holding her mother responsible for this state of affairs, as she explores its meaning for her body as a whole.

During this period, it may feel to the mother as if she can't do anything right for her daughter, as though mom-as-disappointment is the rule of the day. Meanwhile in her daughter's play, bandages often appear on dolls or furniture, as a sign that things need fixing or patching up. A minor scratch becomes worthy of 911. She may even suspend self-stimulation for awhile.

Little boys, meanwhile, respond to the discovery differently. A child may wonder if a penis is really a permanent deal, since he probably recently discovered its absence in females. He wonders, "Since Dad still has his, maybe I need to hang out with him a bit more, and mom a little less to figure out how he keeps his?" Male bonding and action seem to be very reassuring during this era for boys. Children with language can keep us in stitches as they sort this problem out.

Preferential Treatment

Jonathan surprised his mom when he asked her to leave the bathroom as he peed into the potty. "OK, but why?" asked his mom. " I like my penis," was his pithy reply. Was this evidence of some passing theory that "mom-presence" was not in tune with penis appreciation?

Sorting by Gender

As a thinker, the two-year-old adventurer clearly has the ability to categorize his mom, dad, siblings, pets, and the rest of the world into male and female. His memory and past experience, and his own brain have taught him to locate himself in the same gender and to associate with all the pleasures, constraints and privileges of membership in that gender. Socially and culturally, he learns that the feminine is more often associated with comfort and relief of physical and emotional need, and the masculine more often with adventure, risk, and excitement.

By the end of the second year and beginning of the third, this drama begins to play out on a slightly bigger stage. For boys, the father is the first "not-mother" figure of deep significance who is like him. He can be like his dad and assimilate his wisdom and power without feeling too lonely, or pining for his mother, with whom he can no longer be a cuddling, suckling baby.

Girls typically react by moving slightly away from the mother and enjoying the deepening connection with the father at the same time. As she feels affirmed by his attention, she may increasingly challenge her mother's authority, even her femininity: "Daddy likes me better now, Mommy!" is heard fairly often as this stage resolves itself. Advice? Treat it gently, don't mock, and address her feeling that it is nice to have such special feelings for her daddy.

Temperament, Trends and Gender

It would be ridiculous to leave this chapter without reminding ourselves that, at any given moment during development, a child's particular temperament may be a more important factor in his behavior than gender. The same may be just as true for parents.

We also must acknowledge that stereotypes exist for a reason. They come and go across cultures and historical epochs. But parents must remember that gender constrictions generally don't serve their kids well from early on. Mixtures of masculine and feminine traits can combine to give a child's personality greater flexibility and resilience over a life span.

Females did not enjoy equal access to science, mathematics, and technology, the military, politics, or corporate power until fairly recently in our history. Preschools were not immune from such distinctions. One study showed that boys were called upon more often then girls in preschool even though they held up their hands less often. When asked, the teachers felt that calling on the boys was needed to give them confidence. And the 1992 report of the American Association of University Women, "How Schools Shortchange Girls," raised eyebrows by declaring that girls found bias in testing protocols, textbooks, and teacher attitudes.

GUIDELINES FOR MANAGING GENDER-RELATED BEHAVIOR

The two following lists describe behaviors that are more often associated with one gender than the other, though hardly exclusively so. In fact, if a behavior occurs in the other gender, the management advice remains the same.

Girls

Meltdowns: The high emotionality that seems to plague girls more often than boys sets them and you up for frequent trouble, especially in public.

Management: Let her know that you know that she's feeling pretty bad. Then, if you can be heard through the screaming, ask her softly if she's feeling sad or mad. As she settles a bit, ask her if you just need to listen, or does she need help. And then move on. Dragging it out invites more decompensation.

Whining: Not an uncommon behavior.

Management: The trick here is to let her know you do not speak that language and so your "software" is not compatible. "I cannot understand you when you use that voice. Use your regular voice and maybe I can help you." Keep it light, but firm. Consistency is your only hope. The world at large will thank you.

Manipulation: Using a special touch to get special treatment.

Management: As she starts to plead her case, "I know you love Jason more than me, mommy…" stop her right there. There is no point in listening further to the opening argument, because the premise is twisted, and it's a no-win for you. Tell her she'll have more luck with you if she simply says what she needs. You're not guaranteeing results, but you will listen more carefully.

Boys

Impulsivity: Your son shoves the occupant of the chair in front of the computer, unable to wait one more nano-second for his turn.

Management: Tell him you know that it is very hard to wait for something he really wants. But he'll never get it that way. He must wait for his turn. Period. When he does, praise him for his restraint. If he doesn't, he is outta there for the time being with your firm, quiet insistence.

Aggression: At the play group, he grabs the blocks he wants from the kids already using them.

Management: Tell him it hurts other kids' feelings and makes them feel bad to have their stuff grabbed, as it would him. He stops or leaves. If he stops, make a big deal of his self-control. If not, he can't be with the kids for awhile.

Inattention: He's gotten interested in learning his numbers, and you're trying to teach him, but you can't get him to stay still.

Management: Because he's bouncing off the wall does not mean that he's not listening. Boys can sometimes listen better when they are moving. Keep at it and expect him to keep listening whether he is still or not.

But to keep parents on the ball here, I want to say that this pendulum moves pretty fast. While some steps were taken to right these wrongs, now we find that boys are seen as the "behavior problem" and they are facing their own set of biases and having their own troubles. According to a recent *New York Times* article (12/13/98), boys are more likely to repeat grades, be medicated to treat behavior or attention disorders, be placed in special education, or diagnosed with learning disabilities.

Bottom line — boys and girls become who they are as a result of who they and we are together, not by the absence or presence of a Y chromosome. ★

CHAPTER 11

A World of Difference

*How culture, tradition, and family style shape the way
we parent and how our children develop.*

Different-ness inherently fascinates our species. The brain sits up to take notice whenever the unexpected crosses its path. This is especially true from 18 to 36 months. Even infants will turn away from a familiar stimulus once it becomes expected — a phenomenon appropriately called "habituation."

One of These Things Is Not Like the Other

For the toddler or preschooler, things not foreseen hold a special interest. These children spend so much time practicing the put and take, the coming and going — getting good at the predictable — that when the unexpected occurs, they alert and attend with a special acuity. We count on this as parents and teachers, knowing that a new toy or experience is a useful reward or diversion from less productive behaviors. It's a wise traveler who stows a few "new" items to spark interest and shorten the ennui for the long plane or car trip.

Family to Family, Culture to Culture

Different-ness also fascinates at the social level during this era, both in the child and in us. This book's focus on the brain-heart duet would be incomplete, indeed, were we to ignore the differences that define one family from another at both emotional and cognitive levels. We've discussed the power of the unique fit or misfit between a parent's and a child's temperament. But we can *only* understand the uses of that power by knowing the world in which that "fit" lives — i.e., its culture.

By culture, I mean ethnic, racial, religious, socio-economic, geographic, and familial structures, traditions, obligations, and restrictions that encourage or discourage the goodness of that parent-child fit. So, every time you have asked youself throughout this book, "does that apply to *me, my child, my family?*" this chapter will help you decide.

You may think your own daily life is not particularly influenced by cultural variations on child development themes. Yet it is probable that your child will mature in a world influenced more by cultural diversity than the one that shaped you. Our communities, work places, neighborhoods, schools, and families are fast becoming increasingly multicultural.

The opportunities are great. But, as with anything new, there is always the potential for misunderstanding. Each of our cultures has been enriched by the others in everything from cuisine and customs to language and dress. At the same time, we need to know about the values and styles of our neighbors, especially when our little ones are in the company of others whose priorities and behavior are different.

According to the 1995 census, 11.5 million people immigrated to the U.S. from 1960 to 1990. What made this wave different from all previous waves of immigration, such as the largely men-only surge at the turn of the last century, is that these recent immigrants came as families. Another difference is that, after the 1965 Immigration Act, two-thirds of the new arrivals were from Latin and Asian countries. The remaining one-third came from Europe and Canada.

Apart from ethnic diversity, there are other differences that delineate our American families. The structure of the American family itself continues to shift because of changes in length of marriage, age at marriage, frequency of divorce, prevalence of remarriage and reconstituted families, and the use of assisted reproductive technologies. Of all children born in America the last two years of the 20th century, 64 percent will reach the age of 18 having spent some time in families other than those comprised of their birth parents. The nuclear family is a minority in this country, and may have *always* been so, according to some family historians.

A Child's View

These societal changes may seem a peripheral concern for a book on kids from 18-36 months. But in the era when the "self" is first defined in the context of what makes "me" not "you," differences on all levels are fair game for understanding. This is the developmental era in which uniqueness is the royal road to understanding — *without moral judgment, condemnation, or special reverence* — that red hair, almond eyes, quiet demeanor, or skin pigment are fascinating ways to tell one friend from another.

A New Friend

My oldest daughter was 34 months old when the grandson of a family friend accompanied her for a brief visit, giving Lisa her first prolonged, at-home contact with an African-American peer. After a snack, they settled in for some block play and enjoyed each other's company.

An hour or so into the afternoon, Zack came over to sit in front of Lisa and took one of her long brown braids in his hand and asked if it "hurt to get it winded up like that?" "Sometimes," was the reply. Later, Lisa reached up and touched Zack's face with the palm of her hand, and Zack said "What?" After a pause, Lisa said to him "You're warm," and Zack said "Yup." I had no clue what was happening here, as Zack was perfectly healthy. Weeks later, Lisa asked if "warmboy" was coming back to play, being unable to remember his name.

Lisa and Zack were using their three-year-old exploration skills to investigate unique physical attributes in each other — I am, or am not, like that, and that is interesting to me (not good or bad but *interesting*) — devoid of judgment or pejorative intent. Sadly, they would likely encounter such judgments later as they were exposed to forces outside of home that would assign values to those differences. I tell their story here simply to remind us it doesn't start out that way. We have an important window in our children's early years to build a good foundation to guard against prejudice from taking root.

The placement of this discussion in this book is driven by another development inherent during this era. Before 18 months, a child is a passive enough entity, culturally speaking, that most cultural activities around them have to do with rituals that place them inside their particular culture. But as children begin to speak for themselves, they become a force with which to be reckoned, and cultures begin to take active steps to teach the young the verbal and behavioral "language" of their particular culture.

That's why we'll spend some time understanding how this works, because it has potentially great power in shaping the way a child will relate to the world outside the family. To do justice to this topic, of course, would take volumes. But even beginning to open our eyes to the issues that shape some families and their children differently from others seems worthy on behalf of our and their children.

Shaping Cultural Values and Behavior

Children are raised somewhat differently in European-descent, African-American, Asian, Latino, large, and small families. Religious differences within these ethnic groupings further shape attitudes toward discipline, sexuality, and interpersonal behavior in children.

Geography, too, shapes parent-child relationships. This has always fascinated me, coming as I do from a family that roots itself in the South, Midwest, Southwest, West, and now New England. Time, work, distance, neighborliness, trust, openness, and provinciality — like the soil and the light — vary by hues and values from region to region.

Family structure, especially the circumstance of the single-parent family, also sculpts children. Number and order of siblings is another "cultural" honing device. The overachieving eldest, the comfortably dependent youngest, and the partially overlooked middle mediator are common characterizations.

To appreciate the reach of these issues, imagine how families shaped differently by the above forces might approach problems of sleep, social play, excess motor activity, or aggression in the toddler or preschool child. Quite a quilt, is it not?

Cultural Themes and Variations

Ideas, beliefs, and expectations about child development are some of the ways that individual cultures differentiate themselves. Carolyn Edwards of the University of Kentucky studied differences country to country among Japanese, Australian, Lebanese, and New England parents in their developmental expectations for their children. She found:

★ **Lebanese and Australian parents (mothers and fathers) typically had the "latest" or most relaxed expectations regarding reaching developmental milestones of walking, talking, and being able to cooperate with other children. The New England parents had the earliest, or most demanding expectations. The rest remained in the middle.**

★ **Japanese parents had the earliest expectations regarding emotional maturity (not crying readily, mastering one's anger, withstanding disappointment), and the Lebanese and Australian mothers, in particular, had the latest expectations.**

★ **New England parents had the earliest of all expectations in the social domain, whereas the Japanese and Australian parents were more relaxed.**

With regard to specific behavior milestones, Abraham Wolf of Case Western Reserve University found variations in patterns among Caucasian-American, African-American, and Japanese-American families. In the latter two groups, co-sleeping occurred more frequently. These were cultures where grandparents were also more frequently in the home, possibly limiting sleeping space and privacy options. But variations in values of autonomy and independence also play a role here, and cannot be separated from the context in which the co-sleeping arrangement occurs for a particular child at a particular stage of development in a particular household.

African-Americans are, of course, a diversity within a culture. Slave ancestry defines the largest contingent, which itself varies widely between Louisiana, Texas, New England, New York, etc. Carribean Islanders and new immigrants from West and East Africa since 1965 enrich this population further.

For the ethnic group as a whole, certain findings illustrate interesting trends. Davido Dupre of the University of Pennsylvania reports on research that finds black infants and toddlers attain motor milestones earlier than do white infants. African-American households also tend toward extended family membership. A number of people may alternate taking primary responsibility for the care of the child. Consequently, attachment research may not apply at all in this normative matrix of care-taking responsibility. In inner-city populations, father "absence" more typically means "not-necessarily-resident," as most children know, see, and depend upon their fathers on a regular basis.

Asian-American children, too, are representative of a diversity within a culture. Korean, Japanese, Chinese, Southeast Asian, South Asian (India, Pakistan) have arrived in various waves of immigration, especially in this century. After 1965, Chinese-Americans surpassed Japanese Americans as the single largest Asian population. Linguistic, religious, and ethnic differences delineate them with regard to traditional beliefs, values, education, etc.

Stanley Sue of the University of California Los Angeles describes research showing that many Asian-American families within this diversity are more likely to emphasize academic achievement, and less likely to encourage independence, autonomy, and the expression of affection or emotion. Some researchers feel this may be changing, the more time such families spend acculturating to Western norms.

Harvard's Jerome Kagan also has found that Chinese-American infants and toddlers vocalized less, were less likely to smile at external stimuli, and showed more social restraint than European-American babies.

Latino children, too, come from many corners of the Hispanic world, including Mexico, Central and South America, Puerto Rico, and other islands in the Caribbean, and may include Native American roots to their diverse heritages. Mexican-Americans make up the largest group, with Puerto Ricans as the second.

Ian Canino from Columbia University summarizes research that shows that socialization values among Latino groups emphasize obedience, conformity in educational groupings, and following rules. Calm, polite behavior and respect for their elders are goals of many Latino child development principles.

UCLA's William Arroyo adds that Mexican families have very strong values regarding family unity and family relationships in general. The high percentage of bilingual homes in which Latino children are raised sometimes heightens concern about potential language delays among their toddlers and preschoolers. However, the vast majority of normal children exposed to two languages learn both languages equally well and remain fluent for life, although they may *start* speaking later than the norm.

All of these cultures have raised countless generations of happy, well-adjusted, accomplished people. Clearly, human beings thrive as they adjust to the wide variety of behaviors, values, and priorities fostered by different peoples and individual families.

Becoming aware of and respecting these differences is a challenge for all of us. For example, the Asian value of social restraint seems to encourage parents to assist their young in curbing verbal and emotional assertiveness. This means teachers and childcare workers (and other non-Asians) need to be cautious about interpreting Asian children's "shyness" or holding back in group discussion and play as signs that they feel anxious or uninvolved. For them, such behavior may well be valued and considered mature.

Diversity in Family Structures

As if this incredibly rich mosaic of human relatedness weren't enough, the structure of the family *within* each culture can vary significantly. There are many ways extended family members, whether living in the same home or not, care for children. Then, too, many factors in today's lifestyle have great impact on the environment in which children grow up. Our pace of living has quickened, and more children live in family structures that shift over time. But children need love, security, order, and routine as much as ever. These needs can be accommodated in every type of family arrangement. But, in today's world, it can be more difficult to provide those basics in any setting.

Single parenting is very significant because of its potential effect on child rearing and because it is so prevalent in our society. At one time or another, 58% of children live solely with their mothers. Interestingly, homes headed by single fathers are undergoing a startling increase compared to two-parent homes.

The problems single fathers face are similar to those of single mothers with one notable exception — they have more financial security. That alone lowers the anxiety about potential holes in the safety net. However, the loneliness, isolation, exhaustion, and lack of privacy, companionship, and time are cruelly similar. Exhaustion is so frequent because there is insufficient respite from childcare.

Single parents often feel some level of guilt about "imposing" on the child. Whether or not such guilt is rational, it is almost always a factor, even in cases of spousal death. This kind of guilt encourages over-compensation because the single parent may view the child as a "have-not" who has been "wronged" and is owed reparation. This can reinforce the child's natural pre-disposition toward an "emperor" view of the world. And the child comes to believe that he *is* omnipotent and deserves to be. In fact he can't handle *not* being so terrific because, as a child of a single parent, he is "fragile."

Many single parents do a terrific job with their children. But the extra workload is huge, and it deserves our respect and support. Those of us with friends or family who are single parents can help a lot. Networking with and for such parents is life-saving, and creating such networks in some form is always possible. If divorce is involved, non-residential parents need our support to stay close to their kids because that is what their kids need and want, prickly though the situation might be between the adults. Taking an extra child of such a family on an outing or shopping or car pooling may not be that much trouble for you, but could be a gigantic relief to a spent and frayed single parent.

Reconstituted families — those created by remarriage — have their own stresses and strains. Children must acclimate to a new parent and perhaps new siblings. Parents must adjust to their new families and, possibly, to shifting custodial arrangements for children of an earlier marriage. Guilt and over-compensation can occur here as well.

As we saw in Chapter 9, stresses and strains also arise in the context of non-parental childcare. Once again, the root cause is concern that parents don't have enough time with their children.

A New Terrain

The point is that the family experience today has many new features, ones that may be unfamiliar to parents as well as to those they turn to for counsel. The changes in culture and family structure impact each of us in different ways. As explorers in this sometimes unfamiliar terrain, we are asked to cope with the unknown and to find and celebrate the riches around us. This new terrain invites compassion, respect, patience, and understanding.

I close with an invitation to open the eyes and ears to the seasons and diversities of the human family experience. It is a story without end, told to children who will change it forever. ★

CHAPTER 12

Ages and Stages

*How the many facets of growth occur
and mesh chronologically.*

This chapter is about how growth in all the areas discussed earlier in this book occurs and meshes chronologically. "Mesh" is a key word here because developments in cognitive, emotional, and social growth do not happen isolated one from the other.

That said, the big caution concerns individuality. The sheer mass of growth from 18 to 36 months is so great that the ways it can happen are endless. No two children are exactly alike. Not even identical twins. The differences become more pronounced by the day.

I hope this book, with its explanations of *total* development, including the social and emotional aspects, can help parents focus more on the uniqueness of their child and less on the "norms." Among other things, there is so much more to enjoy, appreciate, and be amazed by if you look at your child in this comprehensive way.

A World of Style

The developmental benchmarks of early childhood — the "normal" times when certain skills are supposed to appear — can never do justice to the infinite variety of ways that development actually occurs. Yet it is tempting for parents to compare their children to charts and tables of "average" this or "typical" that. Moreover, comparison is inevitable in many childcare settings where parents can't help but see how their child measures up to others. Concern about early learning can put added pressure on parents to watch for signs that language and cognitive development are "on schedule."

However, from a practical point, timing doesn't mean very much. *The order of development of new skills is more important than the timing of the appearance of any one skill.* Jargon before vocabulary, crawling before walking, sucking before drinking. Children pass through these gateways at vastly different rates.

As long as your child is progressing in each area, it doesn't matter if he is a bit "behind" on something, and, satisfying though it may be, it doesn't mean anything if he is a bit "ahead" on something else. For example, numerous studies have confirmed that the vast majority of children who talk later than average are just as smart and do just as well in school as early talkers. It is perfectly normal for a child's interests and temperament to lead her further and faster in some areas than in others. It is also perfectly normal for these interests to change over time.

Benchmarks can be helpful, provided they are used as general guidelines. If you have concerns, check with your pediatrician. A good rule of thumb: don't let other children's progress get in the way of your respect for the individuality of your child.

That said, there are general patterns that are fairly common. By seeing and understanding the patterns, you can better appreciate and work with the pieces.

Whether your child follows the norms or is all over the map, the factors that fuel growth on all fronts are interlinked. Advances are linked to one another. It is when some combination of physical, mental, emotional, and social developments reach critical mass that advances, such as toilet training, can occur. It is also the interaction on all fronts that fuels steady growth in each.

This chapter on chronology will help you understand these interlinks and the changes that result over short periods of time. It's easier to see the dynamic quality of development this way.

In the process I hope you will gain an even greater appreciation of the astonishing growth of this period. It is like no other in the human life span. Your ability as a parent to guide your child's development also is at its peak during this 18-month period. Your patience, firm guidance, and understanding response to your child's energy and independence, preferences and needs, talents and quirks will profoundly affect the grownup your child is becoming.

Along with the enormity of accomplishment, I hope you will be just as wonder-struck by the uniqueness of the path that your own child follows on this extraordinary journey.

18 to 24 Months —
Exploration and Negativism

The hallmark of this period is the birth of the self — the awareness of "me" versus "not me" in body, heart, and mind. At the same time, your child's growth and the integration of her abilities will soar during this six months. Parents are astounded at the changes and amazed at how each augments the others.

Growth is especially evident in appearance, language, and thinking. Your child will no longer look like a baby. Thanks to an explosive growth in her vocabulary, real conversation begins to happen. And you almost can see the wheels turn in her head as she plans, tackles, and solves increasingly complex challenges.

All this growth is manifested in two powerful ways during this period. First, children move to a new level of exploration, one that uses their new skills and powers. Second, their newfound independence gives rise to negativism — a child's first way to assert that his opinions, feelings, wants, and needs are different from yours.

SIGNS OF THE TIMES

Appearance: The most visible change in the "looks" department will be the transformation from "baby" to "child." The rounded, chubby, baby-fat laden body of the last stages of infancy gives way as limbs lengthen and gain muscle tone, and facial features come into focus. As your child's control over his facial expressions becomes more organized, he will be better able to convey his moods, and your job of reading his cues will get easier.

Physical coordination and skills: The walking, but probably still wobbly, 18-month-old will become much more physically coordinated as the second birthday approaches. At this age, most children's energy seems limitless, and they use it for more daring exploits, often at warp speed. Their fine motor skills, along with hand-eye coordination, improve greatly. As a result, they become more competent and more independent in play, discovery, and self-help activities, such as dressing, eating, and bathing. Competence in these areas, in turn, fuels growing independence.

Cognitive development: Imagination and make-believe are the big new-comers during this six months. But all other aspects of cognitive growth move ahead at full throttle as well, especially short-term memory. As memory and understanding of object permanence grow, your child learns that she can find hidden objects, including people. This ability opens up a new world of play in the many forms of hide-and-seek.

Thinking and reasoning improve dramatically. The trial-and-error method of learning gives way to a more deliberative process as the child learns to think through a plan of action or a way to tackle a challenge. Exploration moves up a level as he is no longer content merely to find out what things are like. Now he wants to learn what things do, what he can make them do, and what skills he can practice on them. He will learn to use objects more efficiently in pursuit of his goals. With better memory and powers of concentration, he will be able to work on projects or activities longer, even come back to them later to "finish."

A child also learns to sort, categorize and classify things by their attributes — shape and color, big and little, loud and quiet, soft and hard. She will make increasingly interesting links among the objects, people, and events in her life as she finds out how things are like and unlike each other. She will learn that, once a thing has a physical property, it tends not to change. For example, blocks stay the same shape.

This discovery has emotional implications as she begins to rely on constancy in her world. She will increasingly count on people to stay the same, too.

This is the basis for profound growth in her relationships as she expects people to act a certain way. It is also the basis for her growing ability to foresee the results of her actions.

At the most sophisticated level, children of this age are beginning to understand concepts, to deal with abstractions, and to understand that other people have different perspectives about how things are and ought to be.

Language: This period is typically marked by phenomenal growth in language, as children graduate from simple phrases to short sentences and an explosive growth in vocabulary. A child's speech literally can't keep up with this growth. Most children at this age understand five times the number of words they actually speak, so don't underestimate your child's language comprehension abilities.

However, language growth varies *widely*. Many children talk much later. Some will develop new words only to lose some others, while other children may plateau for months, showing no visible change. If your child is in any of these categories, rest assured that, within the wide range of normal, there is little correlation between language development and intelligence. Later talkers are generally just absorbed with building other skills.

Social skills: Your child will show big gains in inner awareness and socialization skills throughout these six months. Imitation, especially of adults and older children, is a hallmark of this period. Besides teaching him new behaviors and skills, imitation also fosters a growing awareness that other people have different perspectives.

Your child is now fully aware of herself as a separate being, laying the groundwork for new levels of socialization and play with others. Just as she distinguishes herself from others, she will distinguish "hers" from "not hers." This is when "me" and "mine" become key words in her growing vocabulary.

As she uses objects more efficiently, she will learn to use people as effective resources. In this period, she will increasingly look to others for help when something is beyond her ability — a key step in sharing and developing cooperative behavior.

Emotional growth: Emotions during the 18- to 24-month period are shaped largely by the child's growing independence. He will want to do things by himself, and he will not appreciate those who get in his way.

He will struggle emotionally as he learns to cope with the pull toward the safety of his parents and the magnetic fascinations of the outside world. You will see this as he begins to practice being out of your eyesight for longer periods of time and at increasing distances from you. This is a sign of growth and a necessary testing of limits to make sure they are in good working order. As your child tries to run away from you, bolting down the aisle in the supermarket, he is reassuring himself that, no matter how fast or far he goes, he cannot get beyond the reach of the safety net you provide.

With your guidance, your child will increasingly be able to express a full range of emotions appropriately during this period. He will show pride in his achievements, embarrassment at his mistakes, and shame when his behavior is inappropriate. It is important for you to support appropriate expression of all emotions.

At this age, a child's wish to please and the fear of damaging the parent's love are paramount. These attributes can be a big help to parenting if you use them wisely.

24 to 36 Months — Self-Assurance, Aggression and Sensuality

The frenetic pace and all-over-the-map quality of growth you saw in the first two years of your child's life will moderate. In the third year, growth proceeds in a more orderly fashion as abilities mature. But this growth is just as important as the earlier spurts to shaping the adult your child will become.

In the coming year, watch for growing self-confidence as your child becomes increasingly competent in many skills and able to solve problems on his own. Improved language skills and emotional control open up new levels of social interaction with adults and children. This can lead to occasional bouts of anger or aggression as he learns the rules of play and good behavior. And, just to make things really interesting, gender identity arrives on the scene, with its retinue of wonder, curiosity, and pride. A heady brew!

Most of all, this period is about more and better. More words, self-help skills, interests, friends, games, and ideas. Better self-control, thinking, understanding, motor skills, and manners. The roots of personality, competence, and self-image are growing deep.

SIGNS OF THE TIMES

Appearance: Perhaps the most dramatic change will be in your child's posture. The protruding abdomen of babyhood will disappear as abdominal muscles strengthen so she can stand erect. Legs and arms lengthen, and baby fat continues to disappear. The result is a leaner and more grown-up look. By this age it is normal for children to begin to vary widely in weight and size. As long as your child is maintaining her own rate of growth, there is no cause for concern if some of her friends are bigger or smaller.

Physical coordination and skills: Two-year-olds are well-known for their phenomenal energy and their constantly shifting attention. Rarely does an activity hold their interest for more than a short period, although they can focus on a favorite activity longer. But all this racing around and flitting about build muscle tone, balance, coordination, and flexibility, and movement becomes better controlled and smoother. These skills are essential in themselves, and they are the ticket to more and better exploration. You can pull back a little on your vigilance.

A whole array of new physical play opens up in this year as your child can run and climb easily, pedal a tricycle, and maintain his balance while kicking, rolling, or throwing a ball. Outdoor time in a yard or a park provides a great outlet for his boundless energy, and a good place for ball games that use and build muscles and coordination.

Your child's fine motor skills also will leap ahead, providing new play and creative options. She will be able to use crayons, markers, and paint brushes much more skillfully. She will be able to grasp and turn knobs, handles, levers, and jar lids. And she will be much more facile with stacking or interconnecting blocks.

Cognitive development: Despite the flurry of activity, your child's attention span is actually growing. He can understand and follow more complex instructions, such as those with more than one action step. You will see big gains in his ability to think through increasingly complex activities or projects in advance, figure out solutions, and carry out his plans. Some of his play will also show order and sequence. This will be especially evident when he imitates adult routines, such as getting his teddy bear ready for "work."

As he can think through a plan, so, too, will he become more skilled in foreseeing the effects of his actions — essential for controlling his impulses and inhibiting unacceptable behavior.

He will be able to solve increasingly complex puzzles as he gets better at matching shapes and sizes. As his physical skills and understanding of cause-and-effect improve, he will enjoy everything from operating mechanical toys and pressing buttons on elevators to turning on the lights and starting appliances (heads up!).

Language: While you have mastered your child's special words and pronunciations since she first began to speak, this period will bring great relief to grandparents and others who have had to rely on you as interpreter. Her speech will improve, and they, too, will be able to understand most of what she says. Her sentences will grow longer, up to five or six words. Her grammar will become more complex as she begins to use plural words and pronouns. By the end of this period she will understand the bulk of the words she will need for everyday conversation.

As her thinking and imagining become richer, she will gain the language skills to tell you about her thoughts, feelings, and ideas, opening a whole new world of communication.

Social skills: Kids get better at playing with other children during this year. They still are pretty selfish, but they understand the concept of ownership, and they are increasingly able to share and take turns. It's fascinating to watch children learn how to play together. Give them some running room to learn the ropes. Keep the amount of play time appropriate to their experience with one another, and intervene only when necessary.

Children remain highly imitative at this stage. Your child will faithfully practice what you do, right down to using your words and tone of voice when commanding a teddy bear to wash behind his ears — proof positive of the importance of the example you set.

Emotional growth: "More" and "better" are certainly the hallmarks of emotional growth in the third year. Your child can engage adeptly in more activities, each of which can spark joy, anger, and everything in between. Her passionate desire for control can be grounds for triumph, frustration, and everything in between.

Mood swings are typical and unpredictable as children cope with learning to control how they feel and what they do. Testing limits is an essential part of this learning, and it will be easier for all concerned if you stick with your program, providing consistency, firmness, *humor,* and loving support.

The tug-of-war between your child's attraction to you and his desire to be on his own will be at its peak during this year. One minute he's racing down the aisle in the mall, and the next he's clinging to you with all his strength. These shifts will likely be common, but they point the way to healthy independence. Patience gets put to the test, but in a good cause.

As parents look back from the third birthday party to the second birthday video, they are usually startled to see that their baby became a real person — *her* own person — with a finely honed sense of who she is. Her distinct personality is evident in her words, quirks, intelligence, skills, and emotions. She has become a confident and amazingly competent being. What a difference a year makes.

And then a twinge of sadness... ★

Beyond
Birthday Three

By now, you know your wonderfully competent, lovable, occasionally maddening, particular little person very well. And you probably feel in love with her in ways that you never imagined. This is a good way to enter the next era of life together, because big changes are close by.

An Anxious Honeymoon

True, your child needs you less for physical maintenance than before. The good thing is that you are less physically exhausted. The downside is that the small intimacies of bodily care and feeding are beginning to fade. Emotionally, your child needs you as much as ever but in more subtle ways, because she is now "big" by her yardstick, quite capable of making herself happy (for awhile) without you.

Even more autonomy is coming. Some of the new strivings come with an interesting twist. Just as your child seems to need a little less maintenance from you, he starts picking and choosing friends and intimates more carefully. For those of you with younger kids to raise, this new autonomy can be a relief. For those of you raising your last child, this new development can carry more than a twinge of sadness.

Nevertheless, preschoolers start playing favorites, as they explore their membership in a particular class of humans called either "boys" or "girls," and that includes parents. Fathers and mothers can become instant favorites or pariahs overnight for no reason other than their gender. It is all part of normal development. But as a departing word of well-wishing, I want to share some thoughts about your preparation as a parent for the next era.

The GrownUp Life

In this book we have talked a lot about the linkage between mind and heart, learning and emotion, relationships and competence. *Now it is time to review those very linkages in your own grownup life.* Parental and marital burnout is a common fellow traveler at the end of the third year. It should not be ignored, any more than a lump or a polyp. And it is just as important that you fix it while it is still benign.

It seems to show up now because we finally let ourselves relax a bit, having gotten our kids talking, potty-trained (or at least started), loving and human enough to believe they will at least have a life. But that's when we often begin wondering about our own life, sometimes for the first time in years.

Research on family development shows that marital satisfaction can get perilously low early in the lives of kids because they seem to be such huge energy sinks. Thoughts of "Are-we-having-fun-yet?" guiltily badger mothers and fathers, especially if they keep these thoughts to themselves. If you are *not* enjoying parenting, it may mean that you are working too hard at it. You may be allowing yourself no savor time because you are too busy whipping the process of development into a frenzy. My father's favorite relevant quote here: "Trying to teach a pig to sing is just a waste of time. It frustrates the farmer and really irritates the pig." Return to being a parent, not a driver, and let your child return to growing instead of balking.

As for the marriage or partnership that spawned this kid, it, too, is usually nurtured by a heart-mind connection that requires periodic preventive and reparative maintenance. The three-year or 36,000-mile (stairs, chasing, cruise & snooze, shopping) check-up is critical for long-term endurance, because if that machine isn't purring along, the wheels are going to eventually come off, given the road conditions ahead.

Take time to be together and uncover who you are as adults with minds, opinions, ideas, hobbies, yearnings, and dreams. Date, overnight away, lunch, whatever. Pay someone else to feed or entertain you for a change to reverse the energy flow. Replenishing affection between adults takes conscious effort. Childcare involves so much touching, holding, carrying, bathing, and comforting that adult sensuality and affection can simply get crowded out of a relationship (especially if a child is sleeping in the parental bed appreciable amounts of time). But the replenishment of that affectional and intellectual tie between the adults will be especially important in the years to come when the older school-age child wouldn't get caught dead kissing a parent on the cheek, much less discussing an idea!

Enough preaching. You'll be fine. Meanwhile, celebrate how far you've come together, and whom you have uniquely become together. These have been golden years to savor and adore. None of us would amount to anything without each other, as these three years show better than any others. ★

My best wishes to you and your family,

Kyle

Professional References

★

Brazelton, T. B. (1992). *Touchpoints: Your Child's Emotional and Behavioral Development.* New York: Addison-Wesley

Fraiberg, S. H. (1959). *The Magic Years.* New York: Charles Scribner's Sons

Johnson-Powell, G., & Yamamoto, J. (1997). *Transcultural Child Development.* New York: John Wiley & Sons, Inc.

Kaplan, L. J. (1987). *Oneness and Separateness: From Infant to Individual.* New York: Simon and Schuster

Lieberman, A. F. (1993). *The Emotional Life of the Toddler.* New York: Free Press

Shore, R. (1997). *Rethinking the Brain: New Insights Into Early Development.* New York: Families and Work Institute

Sroufe, L. A. (1995). *Emotional Development: The Organization of Emotional Life in the Early Years.* Melbourne: Cambridge University Press

Caring for Your Baby and Child, Birth to Age 5, The American Academy of Pediatrics, S. P. Shelov, Ed. (1998). New York: Bantam Books

Handbook of Infant Development (2nd Ed.), J. D. Osofsky, Ed. (1987). New York: Wiley

Your Child: What Every Parent Needs to Know About Childhood Development from Birth to Preadolescence, The American Academy of Child and Adolescent Psychiatry, D.B. Pruitt, Ed. (1998). New York: Harper Collins

Index
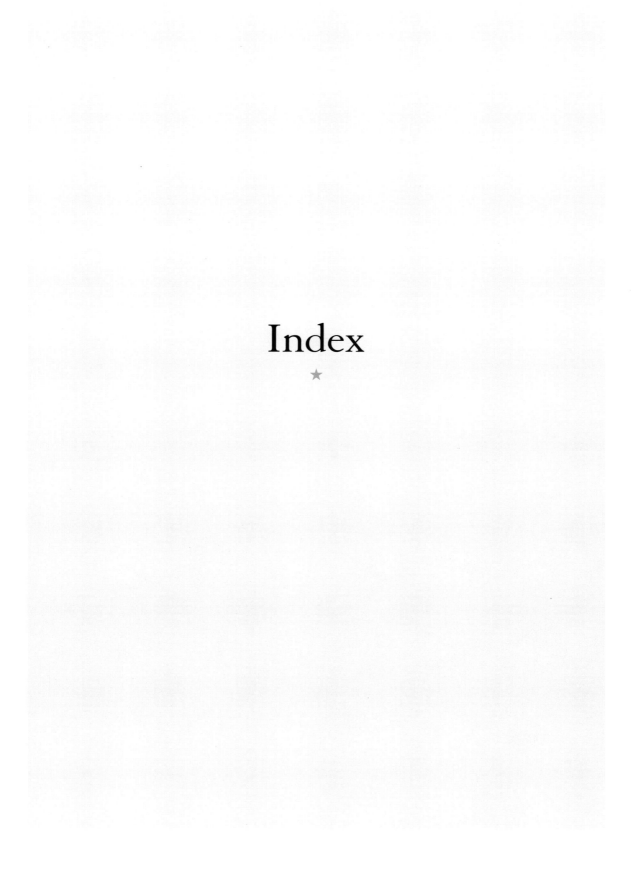

D

M

magnetic resonance imaging, 75

make-believe, 203. *See also* imagination

male bonding, 184

Markman, Ellen, 99

Martin, Earl, 63

memory, 10

    cognition, emotion, and learning, interconnectedness of, 76-77

    development of, 203

    and emotion, 26, 77-79

    and learning, 24

    of limits, 137

    and play, role in, 120

mind, 23-24

    activity of, 18-20, 22

    autonomy of, 53

    development of, 30-32

Minde, Klaus, 67

mind-heart connection, 26, 210-211

moods, biochemical maintenance of, 82

mothers

    disciplinary styles of, 146-148

    interaction with child, and childcare quality, 158

    play styles of, 121

    single parenting by, 197

motivation, 11

    and childcare setting, 159

    frustration effect on, 65

    for skill attainment, 75

    understanding, 143

motor skills

    of 18- to 24-month-olds, 203

    learnplay for, 89

    for play, 120

    of 24- to 36-month-olds, 206-207

muscle development, learnplay for, 89

music, role in imagination, learning, and play, 122-123

N

National Institute of Child Health and Human Development, 157, 161

nature. *See also* genetics

    nurturing of, 4-5, 30-31, 37-38

nature versus nurture, 4-5, 45

needs of child, responding to, 48, 50

negative emotions management, 9, 81, 127, 134. *See also* self-control with play, 114-116

negativism, 127

    emergence of, 132, 202

neurons, 15, 25

neurotransmitters, 25-26

    and behavior, effect on, 40-41

    mood maintenance by, 82

New York Longitudinal Study, 4

"no"

    child's use of, 140

    use of, 57, 136

norepinephrine, 41

novelty, preference for, 3, 80-81

nurturing

    of boys versus girls, 178-179

    and brain development, effect on, 16-17, 22

    and inborn traits, interaction of, 4

    of nature, 4-5, 30-31, 37-38, 45

O

overstimulation, 20

ownership, 62

P

parasympathetic system, 74

parental behavior, 6-7

    during punishment, 145

parental burnout, 209

About the Author

★

KYLE D. PRUETT, MD, is a nationally known child development specialist. He has been a practicing child and family psychiatrist for over twenty years and is a clinical professor of child psychiatry at Yale University's Child Study Center.

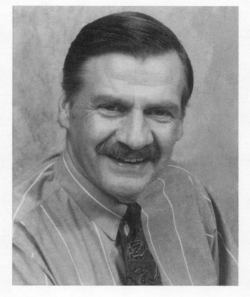

Dr. Pruett has written extensively for national parenting and family magazines on issues of child development, is currently on the editorial board of *Child* magazine, and is a columnist for the AOL-affiliated Website, *Family Education Network*. He is a frequent commentator and contributor to national media on children's issues, and has appeared on most national network news programs and news magazine shows. He hosted his own 26-segment series, *"Your Child 6 to 12 With Dr. Kyle Pruett,"* for Lifetime Television.

He is the president of *Zero to Three: National Center for Infants, Toddlers, and Families,* the nation's leading think tank and information source on young children and families.

Dr. Pruett is also a leading authority on fatherhood and the changing structure of the American family. He is the author of *The Nurturing Father,* published in 1987, for which he received the American Health Book Award and which *The New York Times* called "visionary." He is a Founding Member of Father to Father, chaired by Vice President Al Gore. He is a Presidential appointee and consultant to the Committee on Preschool Children of the American Psychiatric Association.

Dr. Pruett has served as consultant to numerous government agencies, academic institutions, and professional associations. He is the author of over fifty scientific and professional papers.

Dr. Pruett and his wife, Marsha Kline Pruett, Ph.D., have three daughters and live in Guilford, Connecticut.

Also from Goddard Press:

★

Right From Birth
Building Your Child's Foundation for Life
Birth to 18 Months
Craig T. Ramey, Ph.D. ★ Sharon L. Ramey, Ph.D.

A comprehensive guide to raising happy, well-adjusted, successful children *Right From Birth*. In this landmark book the Rameys make sense of the wealth of new research that shows how everything — from personality to early learning ability — is being shaped for a lifetime *beginning in infancy*. They then translate their expertise into "Seven Essentials" — practical steps parents can use every day to raise good-natured, confident, caring, and accomplished children.

★

Going To School
How to Help Your Child Succeed
Sharon L. Ramey, Ph.D. ★ Craig T. Ramey, Ph.D.

A Complete Handbook For Parents of Children Ages 3 - 8 on the all-important transition to kindergarten and the early elementary grades. Based on studies of thousands of children across the country, the Rameys show when and how to prepare children for the move to "big school" and how to support their early and continuing success academically, with teachers and their peers.

CRAIG AND SHARON RAMEY are renowned child development specialists and have done the most extensive work to date on what permanently enhances development in young children. The Rameys direct the Civitan International Research Center at the University of Alabama at Birmingham.